NEW HANOVER COUNTY PUBLIC LIBRARY
DONATED BY:
Friends of the Library
In Honor Of
Vivian Duncan

UNDERSTANDING
THE BLACK MOUNTAIN POETS

Understanding Contemporary American Literature
Matthew J. Bruccoli, General Editor

Volumes on

Edward Albee • John Barth • Donald Barthelme
The Beats • The Black Mountain Poets
Robert Bly • Raymond Carver
Chicano Literature • Contemporary American Drama
Contemporary American Science Fiction
James Dickey • E. L. Doctorow • John Gardner
George Garrett • John Hawkes • Joseph Heller
John Irving • Randall Jarrell • William Kennedy
Ursula K. Le Guin • Denise Levertov • Bernard Malamud
Carson McCullers • Vladimir Nabokov • Joyce Carol Oates
Cynthia Ozick • Walker Percy • Katherine Anne Porter
Thomas Pynchon • Theodore Roethke • Philip Roth
Mary Lee Settle • Isaac Bashevis Singer • Gary Snyder
William Stafford • Anne Tyler • Kurt Vonnegut

UNDERSTANDING The Black Mountain Poets

by EDWARD HALSEY FOSTER

UNIVERSITY OF SOUTH CAROLINA PRESS

Copyright © 1995 University of South Carolina

Published in Columbia, South Carolina, by the
University of South Carolina Press

Manufactured in the United States of America

Library of Congress Cataloging-in -Publication Data

Foster, Edward Halsey
 Understanding the Black mountain poets / Edward Halsey Foster.
  p. cm.--(Understanding contemporary American literature)
 Includes bibliographical references and index.
 Contents: The geography of it—Charles Olson, poetry as politics—
Robert Creely, poetics of solitude—Robert Duncan, aspirations
of the word.
 ISBN 1-57003-014-6

 1. American poetry—North Carolina—Black Mountain—History and
criticism. 2. Duncan, Robert Edward, 1919- —Criticism and
interpretation. 3. Olson, Charles, 1910-1970—Criticism and
interpretation. 4. Creeley, Robert, 1926- —Criticism and
interpretation. 5. Poetry—20th century—History and criticism
6. Black Mountain (N. C.)—Intellectual life. I. Title.
II. Series.
PS266.N8F67 1995
811'.54099756—dc20   94-186

To Elaine

CONTENTS

Editor's Preface ix
Preface xi
  Chapter 1 The Geography of It 1
  Chapter 2 Charles Olson:
                  Poetry as Politics 25
  Chapter 3 Robert Creeley:
                  Poetics of Solitude 81
  Chapter 4 Robert Duncan:
                  Aspirations of the Word 122
Select Bibliography 167
Index 193

EDITOR'S PREFACE

The volumes of *Understanding Contemporary American Literature* have been planned as guides or companions for students as well as good nonacademic readers. The editor and publisher perceive a need for these volumes because much of the influential contemporary literature makes special demands. Uninitiated readers encounter difficulty in approaching works that depart from the traditional forms and techniques of prose and poetry. Literature relies on conventions, but the conventions keep evolving; new writers form their own conventions—which in time may become familiar. Put simply, *UCAL* provides instruction in how to read certain contemporary writers—identifying and explicating their material, themes, use of language, point of view, structures, symbolism, and responses to experience.

The word *understanding* in the titles was deliberately chosen. Many willing readers lack an adequate understanding of how contemporary literature works; that is, what the author is attempting to express and the means by which it is conveyed. Although the criticism and analysis in the series have been aimed at a level of general accessibility, these introductory volumes are meant to be applied in conjunction with the works they cover. They do not provide a substitute for the works and authors they introduce, but rather prepare the reader for more profitable literary experiences.

M. J. B.

PREFACE

Charles Olson, Robert Creeley, Robert Duncan, and other poets associated with the Black Mountain school of poetry have been the subjects of much critical and scholarly attention in the past twenty-five years. Substantial biographies of Duncan and Olson and major studies by distinguished writers such as Paul Christensen, Sherman Paul, and Nathaniel Mackey have been published. George Butterick, Richard Blevins, and Robert Bertholf have provided reliable texts; Olson's *The Maximus Poems* and *Collected Poems* are now available in reliable editions, and Duncan's collected works are currently being prepared for publication. In spite of the attention the Black Mountain poets have received, however, until now no single-volume introduction to their work has been available.

In his introduction to *The New American Poetry* (1960), Donald Allen listed the poets he felt should be seen together as members of the Black Mountain school. There were first Olson, Creeley, and Duncan, all of whom had taught at Black Mountain College. To these Allen added three who had studied there: Edward Dorn, Joel Oppenheimer, and Jonathan Williams. (John Wieners, who was also in the anthology and who had studied at Black Mountain, was for no apparent reason grouped with poets who had "no geographical definition.") Allen also identified Paul Blackburn, Paul Carroll, Larry Eigner, and Denise Levertov as mem-

PREFACE

bers of the school on the grounds that they had published in the group's principal journals, *Origin* and *Black Mountain Review,* although they had no official connection with the college.

In fact, although there are similarities among the works of many of these poets—Oppenheimer, for instance, learned from Creeley's example—their differences in sensibility are often more striking. Even Olson's theories of projective verse, which were Black Mountain's most celebrated contribution to poetics at mid-century, were not universally adopted by the group. Creeley, who was personally as close to Olson as anyone in Allen's list, did not write anything that might be designated projective verse until long after *The New American Poetry* had given him the label by which he has ever since been identified.

What then does the label *Black Mountain* imply? Some critics have used it simply to indicate a loose set of friendships and associations among poets, while others have used it to suggest that vast range of aspirations in the arts, particularly poetry, that one found at Black Mountain College, among other experimental schools, in the 1940s and 1950s. The term *Black Mountain* is obviously imprecise, but it is useful to read the poets on Allen's list in conjunction with each other; they were, after all, intensely aware of each other's work at a time when most academic and professional literary critics still ignored them.

PREFACE

This study centers on Olson, Creeley, and Duncan. All three taught at Black Mountain, were aware of each other's work almost from the beginning of their careers, and worked out their poetics before most of the other poets on Allen's list started writing. Further, they had common ground in an American poetic tradition rooted in theories of Ralph Waldo Emerson. That tradition reached them from very different directions but gave them all, despite their radical differences in personality, sensibility, and general ambitions, a common apprehension about what a poem might achieve. It is the Emersonian alliance among these poets that this study principally affirms.

The first chapter contains a summary of the circumstances that led to the development of Black Mountain as a focus of radical experimentation in American education and the arts and discusses Black Mountain aesthetics and its roots in the works of Ralph Waldo Emerson.

In a chapter on Olson, I consider first the various ways he was influenced by that strain of Emersonian poetics in which, to quote Emerson, "every new relation is a new word." I present *The Special View of History,* Olson's fullest exposition of his poetic and political speculations, in the context of the general development of his poetry from the early formalist and symbolist efforts to the complex postmodernism of *The Maximus Poems.* I also deal briefly with Olson's scholarship in American literature,

PREFACE

particularly his interest in Melville and its consequences for his poetry.

In a chapter on Robert Creeley I place his work in the context of that Emersonian concentration on particulars and the "real" that is found as well in Thoreau, Dickinson, and Stein. The chapter also contains a consideration of Creeley's fiction, which tends to be more adventurous than the early lyrics, although his later poetry, like *Pieces* (1968), is as innovative as the early prose.

In the final chapter, on Robert Duncan, I examine Duncan's association with Jack Spicer and the Berkeley and San Francisco poetry communities in the 1940s and 1950s. I also treat the significance of theosophical and mystical traditions to his work and the ways in which these traditions, together with an Emersonian definition of the poet, drew Duncan to Olson's projectivist poetics. Of all the Black Mountain poets, Duncan, in practice if not always in stated poetics, is most consistently akin to Olson—more so even than Creeley.

I am grateful to librarians at the Bancroft Library, the Columbia University Library, the Kent State University Library, and the New York Public Library. A grant from the National Endowment for the Humanities underwrote my work at the Bancroft. Virginia Admiral, Blanche Cooney, Mary Fabilli, Michael McClure, Richard Moore, Lili Fabilli Osborne, and Eloyde Tovey, among others, contributed materials and insights that helped to shape my perception

PREFACE

of the Black Mountain poets and their work. My discussion of the Duncan-Spicer relationship draws on Lewis Ellingham's massive and as yet unpublished study of Spicer, "Poet, Be Like God."

This book is especially indebted to Sherman Paul, who brought to his work on Olson, Creeley, and Duncan an understanding of Emersonian thought that showed exactly where Black Mountain poetics had their American roots. I have also found Nathaniel Mackey's *Gassire's Lute: Robert Duncan's Vietnam War Poems* exceedingly helpful. His book seems to me by far the best study of Duncan we have; like Susan Howe's study of Dickinson and Olson's study of Melville, it is written with the sympathy and insight of one whose own work is indebted to his subject.

UNDERSTANDING
THE BLACK MOUNTAIN POETS

CHAPTER ONE

The Geography of It

Where a democracy is composed of a people in which the indivitdual conscience and nature is not liberated, so that a common standard or consensus of the majority rules and not the union of each in free volition, the state is already totalitarian.
—Robert Duncan, "The H. D. Book"

It depends on the mood of the man, whether he shall see the sunset or the fine poem.
—Ralph Waldo Emerson, "Experience"

Black Mountain College was founded in 1933, one of the worst years of the Great Depression. The school was in large part the work of John Andrew Rice, who had been dismissed from his tenured position as a professor of classics at Rollins College as a result of a protracted dispute with the president over educational policies and procedures.[1]

Rice joined former Rollins colleagues in raising funds to establish a new college where they could implement their own comparatively radical educational theories. In spite of the country's economic crisis, or perhaps because of it (radical solutions often being particularly attractive at such moments), they soon found the money and Rice and his

UNDERSTANDING THE BLACK MOUNTAIN POETS

associates leased buildings owned by a religious organization in Black Mountain, North Carolina, as the site for their experiment.

One of the most prominent aspects of the new school was its relative freedom from bureaucratic and administrative control. There were no deans, no board of trustees, and no president; decisions were made democratically by the instructors, who selected from their number a "rector"—the post that Charles Olson, among others, would occupy—who led faculty discussions, during which the general business of the school was determined, and who acted as liaison to the world at large. In the actual decision-making, the rector's vote was no more significant than that of any other faculty member.

The school was never very large; it opened with only six faculty members and twenty-two students. In its twenty-three-year history, fewer than twelve hundred students attended, and that figure includes those who came only for a summer session or part of a year.

The poet M. C. Richards, an instructor between 1945 and 1951, pointed out in her reminiscences of Black Mountain that the school operated under overwhelming constraints: the faculty was expected to "teach for almost no salary," while students were asked "to learn without grade points."[2] The very things that motivate the operation of traditional schools were missing, yet proportionate to its size, no college or university in the United States at mid-

THE GEOGRAPHY OF IT

century was able to attract so distinguished a faculty, at least in the arts. Faculty members in the school's final decade included John Cage, Merce Cunningham, Willem de Kooning, Buckminster Fuller, Lou Harrison, Franz Kline, Robert Rauschenberg, Dan Rice, David Tudor, and Stefan Wolpe.

John Andrew Rice was without question the central force in founding Black Mountain College, and his was the primary voice in setting the educational policies of the new school. According to William C. Rice, the founder's grandson, Rice "thought that traditional educators were generally a lifeless lot, authoritarian and unconcerned with the student," and he objected equally to the progressives for "their lack of liberal learning" and their "scientific posing." In general, he criticized higher education for centering on "social or intellectual development" at the expense of the "whole person." [3]

In his memoirs, Rice argued that everyone was born an artist, but while some realized their artistic natures, others were oppressed by the "public world, ready-made, stern, demanding." Black Mountain's task, as he saw it, was to provide opportunities for those who wanted to escape that public world and reassert their artistic nature. The school's principal mission was to help "faltering or even lapsed artists." [4]

Black Mountain was very much an Emersonian project in self-reliance. Rice wanted an institution that would allow

UNDERSTANDING THE BLACK MOUNTAIN POETS

individuals to develop according to their abilities rather than preach the dictates of any discipline or the requirements for particular careers. Rice was himself a perfect, though cantankerous, specimen of the kind of person he hoped to inspire—one who placed personal integrity much above the merits of social or political compromise. Such a person is often in conflict with others, and differences of opinion were in fact behind Rice's resignation from the school seven years after its founding.

In 1937, the college purchased a large tract of land surrounding a lake on the outskirts of Black Mountain. The property had been developed as a summer camp, and there were several rustic buildings set around the lake and in the nearby woods. Initially the school had great ambitions for the land, and Walter Gropius and Marcel Breuer were hired as architects, but their designs proved too costly. In 1940 the starkly modern Studies Building, which was designed by A. Lawrence Kocher, was constructed on one side of the lake, and other, much smaller buildings were later added, but the new campus continued to look like a summer camp—which in fact is what it has become again today.

The school's rustic appearance was actually more in keeping with its character than the ultramodern and institutional Bauhaus design would have been. Without any real center, except perhaps the dining hall or the Studies Building, and with buildings scattered here and there around the lake and throughout the woods, the physical plant seemed

THE GEOGRAPHY OF IT

to emphasize the school's insistence that what mattered was the individual, not some common plan.

Initially Black Mountain took what seemed at the time a particularly liberal attitude toward coeducation. This attitude, however, eroded considerably during Olson's years as rector. In Rice's words, men and woman should learn "that their relationship to each other . . . is to be, in the main, not one of opposites, but of those who live upon the common ground of humanity."[5] During Olson's tenure, an intensely macho attitude prevailed—a point to be emphasized, given the fact that Black Mountain poetry was written almost exclusively by males.

Francine du Plessix Gray, who studied in the early 1950s under the man she called "Big O" (Olson was 6'7" tall), has written about her difficulties as a woman at Black Mountain during his regime. Olson treated women students in authoritarian and patriarchal ways that obviously ran counter to Rice's plans for the school. In fact, in some respects Black Mountain had very early become a male preserve, and while women did serve as instructors, most of the celebrated writers and artists who taught there were male. Among them were Eric Bentley, Ben Shahn, Alfred Kazin, Robert Motherwell, and Josef Albers. Gray was one of few women at Black Mountain at that time, while the list of male writers, both among the students and on the faculty, is impressive by any measure. It included Robert Creeley, Robert Duncan, Ebbe Borregaard, Edward Dorn, Russell

Edson, Joel Oppenheimer, Michael Rumaker, John Wieners, and Jonathan Williams. As Gray wrote, however, Olson's "rebellion against all traditional literary forms, [and] his militant insistence on subjectivity, self-expression, self-exposure" transformed everyone with whom he came into contact. At Black Mountain, Gray said, there was that irony of "male oppressors" who, "by teaching [women] to rebel, may eventually become our liberators."[6] Olson first came to Black Mountain in October 1948 to complete Edward Dahlberg's term as instructor in literature. Dahlberg had begun the semester with great enthusiasm, but the Arcadian atmosphere soon disagreed with him. He found the trees "savage" and left before the end of the second week. Olson, who at that time was living in Washington, D.C., had no desire to commit his life to the woods either, but the school was willing to accommodate him if he would spend three days a month at the campus conducting seminars. He soon found the school's high regard for avant-garde movements in the arts congenial to his interests, and he returned the following summer to teach a course in theater. After that he returned periodically to lecture, becoming a full-time member of the faculty in the summer of 1951.

The school was disrupted by a split between faculty who wanted a comparatively traditional institution and those who, like the rector at that time, Josef Albers, wanted to develop it into a center for the arts. Olson's return to Black Mountain in 1951 and his election soon after as rector

THE GEOGRAPHY OF IT

assured the victory of the second group. But while Albers had sought to shape a center for the visual arts, Olson placed greater emphasis on literature. And there were other, more practical differences. Olson was not one to give great attention to the minutiae of day-to-day operations, and there was soon, in the words of Martin Duberman, "an ever more disheveled physical plant; a place distinctive, in other words, not in endowment, numbers, comfort or public acclaim, but in quality of experience, a frontier society, sometimes raucous and raw, isolated and self-conscious, bold in its refusal to assume any reality it hadn't tested— and therefore bold in inventing forms, both in life style and art, to contain the experiential facts that supplanted tradition's agreed-upon definitions."[7]

Olson was not one to concede casually to another's wishes; he took authority where he found it. During his rectorship, as Mary Emma Harris wrote in her history of Black Mountain, "his control was so great and his personality so dominant that the college . . . [became] identified with his personality and ideas."[8] He had his strong dislikes among writers—T. S. Eliot, for example—and their works were rarely if ever taught. His own courses were in effect opportunities for students to study Big O rather than study with him; at one point, for example, he offered a course called "The Present," which was merely a showcase for his opinions; there was no required reading aside from a local newspaper and the *New York Times*.

UNDERSTANDING THE BLACK MOUNTAIN POETS

According to Duberman, Olson—and Black Mountain College during his reign—stressed the prime importance of the individual and his works, "the 'natural' authority of some men over others (and almost all men over almost all women), and . . . the necessity of leading hot lives and asserting (usually through indifference) the supremacy of man over nature."[9]

Olson's principal intellectual thrust during these years lay in defending the individual as the center of importance in spite of a national culture that seemed committed to reducing people to mere pawns in a market economy. In a series of lectures that he delivered to the school in 1956, published in 1970 as *The Special View of History,* Olson defended the individual with all the conviction and force that had marked Emerson's "Self-Reliance" and Thoreau's *Walden.*

Black Mountain, radical though it was in many ways, was also an Arcadian paradise (its lake fittingly named Lake Eden) much removed from changes taking place in the nation during these years. As a refuge from an America that put great stress on conformity, it represented the survival of an earlier, essentially libertarian politics. Under its aegis, poetry that met with little acknowledgment elsewhere found recognition and sustenance. "Maximus calld us to dance the Man," said Robert Duncan,[10] pointing to Olson's foremost assumption, universally shared by the writers he brought together: namely, that the poem is

THE GEOGRAPHY OF IT

always centered in the individual rather than in a tradition, creed, or community.

The two other figures with whom this study is concerned came to Black Mountain at Olson's invitation. Robert Creeley, with whom he had corresponded since 1950 but whom he had never met before the day Creeley arrived on the campus, began teaching there in the spring of 1954. Creeley left that summer but returned a year later and stayed until February 1956. In 1953, while Creeley was living in Majorca, Olson had asked him to edit the *Black Mountain Review,* which would become a platform for the theories of writing the two men had developed in their correspondence. The first issue featured attacks on Theodore Roethke, who had a substantial following among academics, and Dylan Thomas, who was the most popular poet writing in English at the time. But the magazine, democratic in its criticism, also included Olson's attack on Duncan, "Against Wisdom As Such," to which Duncan would respond for many years. Creeley edited all seven issues of the magazine, the last of which, published in 1957, after the college had closed, was given over largely to work by Jack Kerouac, Allen Ginsberg, and other Beats with whom Creeley was by that time allied.

Robert Duncan first visited Black Mountain in 1939, but his uncompromising anarchism was too strong even for this most radical of schools, and he left the day after he arrived. Eight years later he met Olson while the latter was doing research at the Bancroft Library in Berkeley and concluded that Olson was more a scholar than a poet. Olson's first book of poems, *X & Y* (1948), did not impress Duncan (he threw his copy into the basket), but many years later, the essay "Projective Verse" profoundly reshaped his sense of what a poem could be, and he was soon as close to Olson as Creeley was. Duncan visited Black Mountain again in 1955 and returned in 1956 to teach during the spring and fall quarters. While he was there, he worked on poems that were later published in *Letters* and *The Opening of the Field* and that showed the influence of Olson's poetics.

Whatever Black Mountain's ultimate significance to American literature and American education, it seemed wholly out of place in the conformist Eisenhower years—a period when intellectuals were dismissed as "eggheads" and literature was in the hands of the New Critics, who were much too interested in tracing formal patterns and traditions to understand the postmodernist sensibility Olson and his friends were shaping. The school that had been able to expand and acquire its own campus during the Depression found in the affluent 1950s slight financial support from the outside world, and twenty or so students, at the most, were enrolled at any one time. (In late 1954 there were only nine.)

In the final years before the school's closing in September 1956, Black Mountain had little formal organization

THE GEOGRAPHY OF IT

and few conventional standards, yet expectations for students and faculty remained high. However disorganized the institution must have seemed to visitors, there was a firm hierarchy, based, says Duberman, "on talent, toughness, intelligence and honesty."[11] The air was intense with possibility; Olson was beginning to work on *The Maximus Poems,* and Duncan was working on *The Opening of the Field.*

Olson hoped that even without a campus, Black Mountain would somehow continue in spirit. After the school closed, there was in fact one more issue of the *Black Mountain Review,* and the San Francisco Theater Project, a Black Mountain "satellite," as it was known, outlived the college for a few months. But the school's survival can be found in the vast and continuing influence of Black Mountain aesthetics on American art, particularly poetry.

When Olson first came to Black Mountain, his work was known only to a very small group of readers, but by the time the school folded, he was at the center of a ever-growing community of associates and disciples. Although he certainly had critics among avant-garde and innovative poets, his precedence among them was not greatly challenged until various language poets, especially Barrett Watten, singled him out for attack.

The language poets focus their poetics on the material out of which poems are made—language itself—rather than on its agent, the poet. A central question for these writers is whether Olson, and Black Mountain poets generally, reinscribe romantic poetics. Watten, for instance, attacked what he saw as Olson's "ability to incorporate, almost physically, masses of 'evidence' and yet still come up with the essential scenarios of romantic subjectivity."[12] In the 1980s, Olson became an easy target for those who shared Watten's opinion—a poet, they would argue, written into the canon by virtue of his fame. "One keeps saying 'this is Literature,' " Watten wrote, "and eventually it becomes 'Literature.' "[13] We read Olson, he felt, because Olson is read.

Watten distinguished in his book *Total Syntax* between Olson's *Maximus Poems,* in which "the emotive voice, the 'I,' is perceptible as a person behind the words," and Steve Benson's *The Busses,* in which "a formal argument intervenes to render ambiguous the real location of the speaker."[14] Fundamentally, the question is whether poetry should begin with the poet or with the poet's material. From certain political perspectives, it would seem better for the poet to suppress himself or herself in favor of more politically informed views—in particular, the view that the self is a bourgeois fiction.

Watten's position rests on rational argument rather than on an intuitive, personal response, and the personal is finally, for Olson, the only source of reliable judgment. Watten's coolly reasoned position exists, that is, in the very world Olson denied and to which all his poetry is a re-

THE GEOGRAPHY OF IT

sponse, projecting in its place a poetry that does not ultimately depend on procedures of apparent objectivity, analysis, and categorization. These, in Olson's opinion, were the heritage of Greece and had corrupted the imagination. Watten's attack in no way undercuts Olson if one is sympathetic to Olson's position in the first place. If, on the other hand, one prefers the rational, cool dissections that Watten does so well, his arguments can be convincing. Ultimately, Watten is left with his "claim for technique as the most dynamic approach to writing"—each poem, that is, expressing a particular technique rather than a person—while Olson leaves us with the sense of "a person behind the words."[15]

In a world where personality, as Marjorie Perloff wrote, has become a property of talk shows, technique, with its capacity to disrupt convention, may seem politically the more aggressive and effective alternative for the poet.[16] But it can also lead to exceedingly cerebral, intellectual poetry. Poetry can be valued essentially as a formal process or construction. Watten concluded that Olson's "The Kingfishers" is an "exemplary" poem, "in which an argument between discrete materials and different voices determines the form of the poem," while "the 'bad' Olson" involves "a kind of 'uninterrupted statement' . . . both aesthetically static and politically irresponsible."[17] Watten viewed "The Kingfishers" fundamentally as collage—a modernist experiment in dissonance, disjunction, and the

UNDERSTANDING THE BLACK MOUNTAIN POETS

search for new order as in T. S. Eliot's "The Waste Land"; but Olson was in fact much more ambitious than that, going well beyond Eliot in search of a poetry that was much more than the kind of cerebral construction that a language poet like Watten admired.

There was, in any case, no firm break between language poets and Black Mountain poets for many years. Indeed, the magazine that marked the beginning of the era of language poetry, *This,* which Watten edited with Robert Grenier and which began publication in 1971, the year after Olson's death, confirmed the continuing significance of Black Mountain poetics, particularly in questions it raised about the nature of words. Creeley was especially important to the language poets (Grenier edited his selected poems), although very early they rejected Olson's belief that the poem should be speech-based. Turning away from speech, as Ron Silliman wrote, together with "consciously raising the issue of reference," forced the poet "to look ... at what a poem is actually made of ... language itself."[18]

The chief personal split between Black Mountain poets and language poets occurred at a screening of a film on Louis Zukofsky at the San Francisco Art Institute in 1978. After the film, Watten gave a talk on Zukofsky, in the course of which he asserted that one's life and one's language are separable realities. Turning to Zukofsky's *A,* he discussed the poem essentially as a construction, implying that the words there could be moved around the way a

THE GEOGRAPHY OF IT

carpenter moves lumber and nails. Duncan intervened, arguing that he "in no way believe[d] that there is such a thing as 'just language,' any more than there is 'just footprints.' " Rather, "it is human life that prints itself everywhere in it and that's what we read when we're reading."[19] Using Zukofsky's *80 Flowers* as evidence, Duncan demonstrated that Zukofsky was not a poet of impersonal constructions.

A fundamental split between two branches of the American avant-garde had been defined, and in Duncan's view, there was no way to heal the breach. Interviewed in 1985, he compared the language poets to "a crowd of mosquitos off there in someone else's swamp." Whatever their poetics might owe to linguistics, they were "reductionist," he said. Language poets were practitioners of "illogical negativism."[20]

Language poets and Black Mountain poets diverge in the precincts of epistemology. The first group argues that meaning is primarily a product of language rather than of those who use language; or, to put it another way, in great measure we are formed (and thereby achieve our respective identities) through the language we use. Language, furthermore, is generally understood by the language poet as manifestly ideological in nature and function, shaping thought and behavior in ways of which the subject may well not be aware. Language, that is, victimizes the subject, and the language poet is a missionary of sorts, exposing the manipulative power of language, its ability to shape the individual ideologically.

"According to many Language poets," wrote George Hartley, "the voice poem [as developed in Black Mountain poetics, among others] depends on a model of communication that needs to be challenged: the notion that the poet (a self-present subject) transmits a particular message ('experience,' 'emotion') to a reader (another self-present subject) through a language which is neutral, transparent, 'natural.' "[21] It is not the subject (the poet, that is, or the poet's "voice") that speaks but language itself, and this in turn is what language poetry foregrounds, reminding the reader or listener that what he or she encounters has its source in words, not in the person who put them on paper.

Black Mountain poetry, particularly Creeley's, is much concerned with language as such, but language as understood to be fundamentally expressive, rather than constitutive, of those who use it. Meaning, that is, has its beginnings in the poet as intimately as in the words. Hence while the language poet operates within a scenario of victimization, Olson spoke of poetry in terms of "push," "projective," and "projectile"—characterizing energy from the poet that is passed to the reader. A key text for Olson, as cited by Creeley in the context of an essay, is a statement that Alfred North Whitehead made in *Process and Reality:* "There is nothing in the real world which is merely an inert fact. Every reality is there for feeling: it promotes feeling; and it is felt."[22] Whitehead placed the perceiving, feeling indi-

THE GEOGRAPHY OF IT

vidual at the center of the universe. The source of feeling, in his view, is within the self, not the world—or, for that matter, in its language.

Whitehead gave Olson's poetic practice a logical base—a way to justify poetry that is centered in the self but does not merely reassert a romantic ego. Black Mountain poetics quite explicitly rejects romantic conceptions of the self as an ego battling the world or as a passage to divine transcendence.[23] Olson had no use for latter-day romantics like Sylvia Plath and others rediscovering Shelley's "thorns of life" or for the mystics and would-be mystics of the 1960s who used poetry to celebrate a drug-induced transcendent union with the All.

Olson, Creeley concluded, insisted "that he was not involved in some self-aggrandizement and that *The Maximus Poems* were not therefore a backdrop for himself as quondam hero."[24] Nonetheless, he believed, words depended for their life on the presence of the individual, and it was within the individual, identified as a particular physiological and psychological being, that the poem had its source. Poetry depended for its life on the rhythms, music, diction of the individual poet. This was a question not merely of mannerisms or technique but of something much deeper, unique to the poet, and evident in the poet's speech.

In "Against Wisdom as Such," Olson argued that "wisdom, like style, is the man"—rather than, for example, a body of stable or durable truths.[25] For him, as for Creeley and Duncan, wisdom could exist only in the moment and the act of its apprehension. Certainly there was no Platonic universe of ultimate truth. Olson insisted that the poet could not be a member of a particular sect or adopt particular symbols; to do so would be to make poetry ancillary to religion. In one form or another, that argument had been made many times before. As Emerson wrote in "The Poet," "mysticism consists in the mistake of an accidental and individual symbol for an universal one," whereas "all language is vehicular and transitive, and is good, as ferries and horses are, for conveyance, not as farms and houses are, for homestead."[26]

Black Mountain poetry is located in time; in the occasion of its composition; and, above all, in the physiological and psychological identity of the poet. These qualities have long defined the dominant American innovative or avant-garde literary movement. It is, in Philip Rahv's famous distinction, the difference between the Redskin and the Paleface: the latter's work is more likely to respect traditional form and restraint.[27] Both extremes have their dangers. The Redskin at the worst may veer toward adolescent banality and mere self-expression; while the Paleface, working in an outworn aesthetic, may produce only decorous, genteel, or academically precise work. The Paleface—Henry James, for example, or Robert Frost—is temperamentally conservative, whatever his or her formal politics, and more apt to please those who are disconcerted

THE GEOGRAPHY OF IT

by anyone who strays far from the rules. Richard Wilbur is an obvious example of a major contemporary poet whose work depends on prosodic conventions. The New Formalists belong as well to the Paleface tradition.

The Redskin, on the other hand, insists on the unique moment of creation, of which the poem is itself an enactment or reenactment. In addition, most poets in this tradition, and all of those associated with the Black Mountain school of poetry, assert the absolute priority of the poet's self at least as the source of the poem's cadence, music, and structural integrity. The poem may not say what the poet wants (the words themselves will determine whether it does or not), but it will draw on the poet's sensibility for the manner of its expression.

This division between the two poetic possibilities can be found in Emerson. In his early work, he justified his poetics with the concept of correspondence, according to which, to quote his summary in *Nature*, "particular natural facts are symbols of particular spiritual facts."[28] That notion is rooted in antiquity and can be found in the works of a vast range of writers from Jacob Boehme to William Blake, but Emerson's immediate source was Swedenborg, for whom it became a central theological doctrine. Robert Frost, who was brought up in the Swedenborgian Church, accepted the doctrine, and in his view, poetry became the natural means through which higher or moral truths are seen. The individual's special gift, for Swedenborg, the

UNDERSTANDING THE BLACK MOUNTAIN POETS

early Emerson, and Frost, is the ability to see the points at which heaven and earth are one. As Emerson's friend Christopher Pearse Cranch wrote in "Correspondences," "All things in nature are beautiful types to the soul that can read them; / . . . Every object that speaks to the senses was meant for the spirit."[29]

Emerson's great contribution to the doctrine of correspondence—a contribution of the utmost importance for American poetry—lies in his belief that matter and spirit are both perpetually changing; change is the fundamental law of the universe. In place of poetry as a guide to moral laws, this implied a poetry of continual unfolding or process—a poetry in which, as he said, "every new relation is a new word." This concept gave each poet the liberty to pursue poetry in his or her individual fashion, and the result was a great delta of possibilities, of which Black Mountain poetry is one prominent branch.

Emerson led by one route to Thoreau's examining the particularities of life at Walden and recording the data meticulously in his journal, and to Dickinson's refusing the remedies of religion while attending to the most sensitive discriminations between words. But by another route he led to the idealist imaginings of Whitman, who viewed the life of the city with precision but then transformed what he found into vaguely defined, if strongly felt, utopian visions of democratic camaraderie. Similarly, there are, on the one hand, the precise Thoreauvian or Dickinsonian scrutinies

THE GEOGRAPHY OF IT

of Creeley's work, documenting a continual reengagement with the world as it unfolds before us, and, on the other, visionary transcendences in Duncan's. In both, however, the poetry is not bound to absolute forms, mores, or truths; and the poet is free to track change either in its large harmonies or in the particularities of the world. Both kinds of poetry are deportments within the same continuum, the final issue of which is a rejection of artifice, a rejection of presumptive authority, and a rejection of the belief that an established order is preferable to actual engagement with the fact of change.

As Duncan pointed out in an interview published in *Contemporary Literature* in 1980, the Black Mountain school of poetry had its roots in the late 1940s and was well defined by 1960. But by the time of that interview, the movement was "no longer current."[30] Other groups, particularly the language poets, were seeking the attention Olson, Duncan, and Creeley had received a few years earlier. If Black Mountain had lost its force as a movement, however, it left behind a number of younger poets who had clearly learned from it and who are at present among the most closely watched and admired of contemporary poets—Susan Howe, Nathaniel Mackey, Alice Notley, Clark Coolidge, and Gustaf Sobin among many others. The publication of Olson's *The Maximus Poems* (1983) and *The Collected Poems* (1987), Creeley's *The Collected Poems: 1945-1975* (1982) and *The Collected Prose* (1984), together with the collected edition of Duncan's work now being edited, indicates Black Mountain's continuing importance. There have, in addition, been editions of selected works by Creeley (1991), Olson (1993), and Duncan (1993). Whether or not the movement is "current," its influence runs so deep in contemporary American poetry that it remains one of the principal sustaining poetics among innovative poets today.

Notes

1. He was exonerated in an investigation by the American Association of University Professors.

2. Quoted in Mervin Lane, ed., *Black Mountain College: Sprouted Seeds* (Knoxville: University of Tennessee Press, 1990) 11.

3. Lane, 11.

4. Lane, 12, 13.

5. Quoted in Mary Emma Harris, *The Arts at Black Mountain College* (Cambridge: MIT Press, 1987) 7.

6. Quoted in Lane, 301, 311.

7. Martin Duberman, *Black Mountain: An Exploration in Community* (New York: Anchor, 1973) 336–37.

8. Harris, 178.

9. Duberman, 407.

10. Robert Duncan, *The Opening of the Field* (New York: Grove, 1960) 9.

11. Duberman, 407.

THE GEOGRAPHY OF IT

12. Barrett Watten, *Total Syntax* (Carbondale and Edwardsville: Southern Illinois University Press, 1985) x.

13. Watten, 1.

14. Watten, 123.

15. Watten, 123.

16. Marjorie Perloff, *Radical Artifice: Writing Poetry in the Age of Media* (Chicago and London: University of Chicago Press, 1991).

17. Bob Perelman, ed., *Writing/Talks* (Carbondale and Edwardsville: Southern Illinois University Press, 1985) 158.

18. Ron Silliman, "Language, Realism, Poetry," *In the American Tree* (Orono, Maine: National Poetry Foundation, 1986) xvi.

19. Reported in De Villo Sloan, "'Crude Mechanical Access' or 'Crude Personism'; A Chronicle of One San Francisco Bay Area Poetry War," *Sagetrieb* 4 (Fall/Winter 1985): 244.

20. Michael André Bernstein and Burton Hatlen, "Interview with Robert Duncan," *Sagetrieb* 4 (Fall/Winter 1985): 127.

21. George Hartley, *Textual Politics and the Language Poets* (Bloomington and Indianapolis: Indiana University Press, 1989) xii.

22. Robert Creeley, "'An Image of Man . . .': Working Notes on Charles Olson's Concept of Person," *The Collected Essays* (Berkeley and Los Angeles: University of California Press, 1989) 145.

23. Charles Olson, *Human Universe and Other Essays* (New York: Grove, 1967) 59.

24. Creeley, 134.

25. Olson, 68.

26. Ralph Waldo Emerson, *Essays: Second Series* (Boston and New York: Houghton Mifflin, 1883) 37.

27. Philip Rahv, "Paleface and Redskin," *Literature and the Sixth Sense* (Boston: Houghton, Mifflin, 1970) 1–6.

28. Emerson, *Nature, Addresses, and Lectures* (Boston and New York: Houghton, Mifflin, 1883) 31.

29. Christopher Pearse Cranch, "Correspondence," in John Hollander, ed., *American Poetry: The Nineteenth Century* (New York: Library of America, 1993) I, 590.

30. Jack R. Cohn and Thomas J. O'Donnell, "An Interview with Robert Duncan," *Contemporary Literature* 21 (1984): 525.

CHAPTER TWO

Charles Olson:
Poetry as Politics

Nature is chance.
—**Friedrich Nietzsche,** *Twilight of the Idols*

By 1945, Charles Olson was a highly visible and, it seemed, ambitious figure in the Roosevelt administration and the Democratic Party. A prestigious future in government was almost certainly his if he wanted it, but not liking Truman, who was elevated to the presidency when Roosevelt died in the spring of 1945, Olson abandoned politics. Six years earlier he had as abruptly abandoned graduate work at Harvard before completing his Ph.D., although he was by that time deeply admired by some prominent scholars for his work on Melville. In *American Renaissance* (1941), his former professor F. O. Matthiessen, at the time one of the most influential academic critics of American literature, had acknowledged his own debt to Olson's work.[1]

Call Me Ishmael, the book on Melville that Olson completed soon after he left politics, was filled with assertions for which he offered little support outside personal conviction. It was not a book designed to please a traditional academic like his erstwhile mentor, however much Olson had previously enjoyed Matthiessen's respect. When the manuscript was submitted to Harcourt Brace,

CHARLES OLSON

Matthiessen, who had been retained there as a reader, expressed strong reservations about it. Harcourt turned it down.

Call Me Ishmael was modeled on highly personal and idiosyncratic works like D. H. Lawrence's *Studies in Classic American Literature* (1923), William Carlos Williams's *In the American Grain* (1925), and Edward Dahlberg's *Do These Bones Live?* (1941). Academics like Matthiessen seemed radical within their profession, but their scholarship and criticism maintained at least an appearance of impersonality.

There was resistance in English departments to admitting Whitman and Melville into the curriculum with Chaucer and Pope, and it was clear that if American literature was to be accepted in the discipline, it would have to stand up to the seeming impartiality and objectivity of critical analysis. The impersonal tone of Matthiessen's work (compared to Lawrence's, at least) may have helped American literature gain respectability in the university, but the veneer of impersonality and objectivity involved a compromise that Olson, for whom Melville was now a figure of enormous importance, would not make. His belief in Melville's greatness was a matter of personal conviction, and conviction, rather than critical impartiality, was where he felt good scholarship began.

After abandoning academia and politics, Olson felt free to speak candidly when he wanted (sometimes to the

POETRY AS POLITICS

distress of those he decided to discuss in public), and from that time forward, he refused exactly such accommodations to academic taste and values as those that, in his view, compromised Matthiessen. In spite of this, Olson remained in many ways an academic, unlike some of the poets with whom he was associated; but he wanted scholarship and criticism that were manifestly personal, not camouflaged by the tones of dispassionate discourse. His most sophisticated theoretical work, *The Special View of History* (1970), initially presented as a series of ten lectures at Black Mountain College in 1956, is a defense of scholarship grounded in the intuitions of the individual.

Olson's theoretical works are among the most highly articulated manifestos and essays in the mid-century struggle to turn American poetry from the traditional work approved in the academic establishment to the range of expression possible in what Donald Allen called "the New American Poetry."[2] Other poets might diverge from Olson in the specifics of poetic practice, but they could find in him justification for believing that their own poetic intentions were, at least for themselves, superior to whatever models the academy was promoting.

"I am willing to ride Melville's image of man, whale and ocean," wrote Olson in *Call Me Ishmael,* "to find in him prophecies, lessons he himself would not have spelled out."[3] That willingness gave Olson the license to elaborate a highly personal vision that, whatever it may or may not

CHARLES OLSON

have said about Melville, provided the ground on which Olson could erect his own theories of poetry. At the center of his vision was the notion that the route to the universal is through the particular—not an unusual claim, but one out of which Olson developed a highly individual and influential poetics. As he saw it, "the intimate and the concrete of the present . . . enabled [Melville] . . . to loose [sic] himself into space and time and, in their dimensions, to feel and comprehend such an object as the Pyramids, to create, in like dimensions, an Ahab and a White Whale" (*CMI,* 101).

Whatever Melville actually comprehended when he confronted the pyramids (it was in fact one of his most sublimely nihilistic moments, culminating in the assumption—as it happens, incorrect—that the Judeo-Christian god could be traced to Egyptian death worship), Olson too was setting out to discover ways "to loose himself in space and time"—to be free of the corrupt politics, the conventions of academic life, and whatever other constraints might impose themselves. That search would culminate in *The Maximus Poems,* which opens in Gloucester, Massachusetts, where Olson had spent summers as a child and where he returned to live in 1957, but moves rapidly to the revelation of what the speaker, Maximus, considers an ideal "polis."

The poetry Olson wrote before 1945 was much too observant of convention and restraint to permit such freedom. "White Horse," for example, a poem from the early

POETRY AS POLITICS

1940s, is a formalist exercise in rhymed quatrains. It is the kind of work one could expect to see used as a filler in popular magazines of the day. Certainly it was not a poem that its readers might find particularly disturbing or unusual. Its subject is desire; male desire is symbolized by a white horse and female desire by a black one:

> He grew more human,
> less woman she,
> image approached
> animality.[4]

Olson forces the poem into metrical conventions, and he does so with great skill. The stanza is cleverly written, but one is aware of its technical restraints at all points. The success of the poem depends on grace and musicality in spite of rigid formal demands. A feat like this corresponds in a general way to literary criticism in which one discusses and defends Whitman or Melville without ever confronting or expressing the personal reasons for one's enthusiasm. Formality dominates.

Olson's early poems repeatedly indicate that, had he chosen, he could have established himself as a traditional poet much like those that critics, turning from the more political verse of the 1930s, were beginning to admire. These poems give little indication of those which he would write a few years later and which were usually published, when they were published at all, in places like *Harper's Bazaar,* that would retrospectively seem odd in view of his later reputation.

"The House," written about the same time as "White Horse" is slightly less traditional in form (it is a prose poem in five paragraphs) and evokes exactly the kind of self-absorbed "poetic" experience that Olson would sweep away in his definitive 1950 essay "Projective Verse." In effect, the poem says no more than Rousseau had said two hundred years earlier, expressing a sentiment that had become in the meantime a romantic cliché: we are alone among many people, unable to communicate, and we feel our solitude deeply.

"The K," written in 1945, when Olson was in the process of going beyond the conventional limitations of his earlier work, addresses the reader in the direct, firm voice that characterizes much of the later poetry. Written as a declaration of independence when, as Olson's biographer Tom Clark wrote, the poet had abandoned his political career, it asserts the importance of sexuality over politics and the affairs of the world, particularly those of the "romans," Olson's term for Washington bureaucrats. The poem's directness and wit are weakened, however, by the conclusion, which returns to the symbolic mode of "White Horse" in a list of four objects by which the speaker wants to be identified: "a bridge, a horse, the gun, a grave."

Nearly a quarter of a century later, Olson would end *The Maximus Poems* with a very different kind of list:

POETRY AS POLITICS

   my wife my car my color and   myself[.][5]

This list was drawn from the poet's literal, daily world, whereas the 1945 list that ends "The K" consists of a group of symbols, less important for the specifics they name than for the qualities and abstractions they suggest. The horse in the list in "The K," for example, may be intended as a symbol of male desire, as it had been in "White Horse"— although that may not be the case, the problem of interpretation (or the virtue, as Stéphane Mallarmé argued) being the very diffuse and indefinite field of reference that a symbol may establish. The list is conventionally "poetic," even though most of the rest of the work suggests that its writer was undergoing a radical shift in his ambitions as a poet.

Before 1945, the scholar, politician, bureaucrat, and poet, Charles Olson had accommodated himself to other people's expectations and ideas. Whether investigating Melville's sources, teaching undergraduates, playing a role in the Roosevelt administration, or writing verse for *Harper's Bazaar,* he assumed identities from the world at large and was in every case successful. In 1932, as a promising young scholar, he had entered the graduate program at Wesleyan University, where he had done his undergraduate work. The subject of his master's essay, titled "The Growth of Herman Melville, Prose Writer and Poetic Thinker," had been unusual, since Melville had not yet been accorded major status in the canon. The methodology too had been unusual: at his adviser's insistence, Olson had ignored all earlier critical work on Melville. But in writing the essay, Olson had still identified with traditional academic expectations.

In contrast, in "Letter for Melville 1951" ("written to be read AWAY FROM the Melville Society's 'One Hundredth Birthday Party' for MOBY-DICK at Williams College, Labor Day Weekend, Sept. 2–4, 1951"), Olson savagely attacked professional Melvilleans and their genteel conference ("This abomination, . . . the false & dirty thing which it is"). Melville scholarship, he said, was a means for their own advancement and pleasure, using "a dead man's hand" to "scratch each other's back" (*CP,* 233, 234). Olson did not build a career in the way they had done, but at first his interests and methods had initially been as orthodox as theirs.

Demonstrating his legitimacy as an academic, Olson had immersed himself in one of the most traditional of all concerns in literary scholarship—the influence of one writer on another. Rather than simply conjecturing what could have led to *Moby-Dick* ("the intimate and the concrete of the present," and so on), he had set out to identify Melville's exact sources. This had led to the discovery of volumes from Melville's private library and, most significant, his set of Shakespeare, which gave Olson proof that it had been Shakespeare's work, particularly *King Lear,* that had been the catalyst in Melville's transformation from a

POETRY AS POLITICS

writer with an eye on the market into the author of *Moby-Dick*. As Olson wrote to the Melville scholar Merton M. Sealts, Jr., many years later, sources were the essential matter on which the study of Melville turned.[6]

Sources are important too in studying Olson's work, but in a very different way. Olson was an prodigious autodidact, but he often used his readings essentially to substantiate what he already believed to be true. As the academic that he certainly was, however unorthodox, he clearly must have recognized the virtue of grounding his speculations in arguments that had already been accepted by scholars and critics. He conventionally used other writers to support or amplify positions he wished to argue. Having disentangled a number of strands woven into Olson's work from his reading, Michael Bernstein concluded that he was "increasingly convinced that a consideration of topology, Riemannian geometry, or quantum physics, contributes surprisingly little to an understanding of *The Maximus Poems*."[7]

And yet it was obviously and obsessively important for Olson to find conceptual agreement between his poetics and, say, the work of the physicists Niels Bohr and Werner Heisenberg. Whether in fact the agreement was there (and there were those who argued with him on this), Olson inherited from Ezra Pound a belief in "paideuma," named by the anthropologist Leo Frobenius and described by Pound as "the mental formation, the conditionings, aptitudes of a given race or time."[8] In designating the points at which his poetics and other disciplines seemed to converge, Olson tried to validate his work as truly contemporary.

It is interesting on this score to compare Olson with Henry David Thoreau, who also tried to confirm his essentially moral and metaphysical positions through the science of his era. Thoreau took geology and botany, which in his day were largely sciences of observation and classification, and added to them a moral dimension, arguing that the exact seeing these sciences entailed could reveal to the trained eye facts about the moral as well as the physical universe. *Walden, The Maine Woods,* the journals, indeed all of Thoreau's major work is largely one long record of what he saw. For Olson's generation, however, science had less to do with microscopes and classification than with the abstractions of mathematics. Olson therefore turned to the geometry of Georg Friedrich Bernhard Riemann, who rejected Euclidean geometry and laid the mathematical foundations for the general theory of relativity. Reimann, as Olson wrote, "define[d] the real as men since have exploited it."[9] But unlike Euclid's universe, which was Thoreau's as well, Reimann's cannot be seen; it is represented symbolically rather than presented through the sensual world of solidities and hard edges.

Thoreau's science was a science of nouns. Accepting the notion of correspondence, he looked to specific facts and events for confirmation of higher truths (a thawing

POETRY AS POLITICS

embankment, to choose a well-known example, as representative of the workings of nature). But the real as defined by Riemann does not have such sharp physical or geographical lines, and Olson is "difficult" at times precisely because he is not visual or concrete in the way Thoreau could be. Olson needed a language as fluid as Reimann's universe, and that is what he found in a poetry that could suddenly become abstract and learned. What mattered was maintaining the "push" or "energy," to use his own terms, of intellectual excitement:

> In English the poetics became meubles — furniture—
> thereafter (after 1630
>
> & Descartes was the value
>
> until Whitehead, who cleared out the gunk
> by getting the universe in (as against man alone
>
> & <u>that</u> concept of history (not Herodotus's,
> which was a verb, to find out for yourself : . . .
> <div align="right">(<i>MP,</i> 249)</div>

One of the principal difficulties that concerned Olson in both his work and his vast reading was the problem of history—the need to find efficient cause or causes for the processes of civilization. He wished to discover, in effect, the roots for the paideuma. His study of Melville's sources implied a linear, simplistic model, one writer providing foundations for the next, but Olson increasingly sensed that history operated in much more complex ways. The solution was suggested by Melville, who led him to believe that history was grounded in the self. By clearing from speculation all gods and all metaphysical systems, Melville left himself with a universe of contingent meanings and no conclusive authority except *personal* authority. Further (and here Olson came upon a notion that would guide his mature poetry), the "application of intelligence to all phenomena . . . [is] *the* ordering agent" (*HU,* 112). The grand, ultimate source for history and the paideuma, that is, was not in institutions, customs, or laws but in the self.

That way of seeing history had been promoted conservatively in the new doctoral program in American civilization at Harvard in which Olson enrolled in 1936. This program, which would become one of the foundations of the American studies movement, merged literature and history, reading the first as a guide to the second. Matthiessen, for example, would claim that "an artist's use of language is the most sensitive index to cultural history."[10] He was obviously granting authority to a very limited group of individuals, but they were *individuals,* after all, while much of the rest of academia, and the country, for that matter, found authority in impersonal forces, whether traditional institutions or the inexorable economics of classical Marxism.

POETRY AS POLITICS

Art in the 1930s was certainly much more than proletarian novels and social realism, yet Matthiessen and his colleagues in the American civilization program were going against the tide by selecting a few elite writers as their authorities. Whitman was enormously popular in this decade as a spokesman for democracy (or socialism, depending on one's politics), the author of poems everyone could understand. Matthiessen, however, saw him as a thinker of some sophistication. The American civilization program and the *New Masses* were not speaking the same language.

In the 1930s, with the country deep in an economic crisis, great value was placed on documentary and factual evidence. In the arts there was a turning away from the experimentalism of the 1920s: social realist painters like Thomas Hart Benton and Ben Shahn, for example, supplanted Arthur Dove and Charles Demuth in the public regard, and the avant-garde little magazine *transition* gave way to *Partisan Review*. The elitism implicit in much of the experimentalism of the 1920s (for only initiates were likely to understand what was involved) was replaced by a concern for regionalism, folklore, and the "common man." Carl Sandburg published several volumes of his account of the life of his archetypal commoner Abraham Lincoln; Aaron Copland composed his *Fanfare for the Common Man;* and Frank Lloyd Wright, most of whose patrons until this time had been among the country's wealthy elite, began to design "Usonian" houses for families with modest incomes.

CHARLES OLSON

Superficially, given Olson's working-class background, it might seem that he should have been pleased with the shift of emphasis to the common man, but his politics would prove more complex than that. His ideal polis would be composed of people who were in one sense absolutely equal—a community in which authority was invested in each citizen individually—yet personally he could be, as Francine du Plessix Gray remembered, authoritative and overbearing.

Olson was born in 1910 in Worcester, Massachusetts, a manufacturing city. His father, a Swedish immigrant, was a letter carrier. He had converted to Catholicism when he married Olson's mother, Mary Theresa Hines. Both of her parents were Irish. Although Olson did not deny his background (it enters often into the poetry), he was much too independent to identify fully with it.

At the same time, he was excluded by religion and ancestry from the Protestant upper class that controlled the business and financial life of the major cities. The history of New England—the Massachusetts Bay Colony, the Boston Tea Party, the battles of Lexington and Concord—was preeminently the history of that class. The major towns and cities all had their historical societies; one of the most famous, the American Antiquarian Society, was located in Worcester.

The American civilization program at Harvard was a counterweight to the antiquarian's genteel and self-serving

POETRY AS POLITICS

image of the past. Many of those involved in the program, like Matthiessen and William Ellery Sedgwick, had good New England pedigrees, but within their own culture they were rebels, advocating Whitman over Longfellow, Thoreau over Lowell, Hawthorne over Holmes. Olson's graduate work at Harvard gave him the opportunity to discover, through writers like Melville, something darker than, and implicitly critical of, the genteel view embodied in the official version of the New England past. But the Harvard program, as extreme as it must have appeared in some quarters, was still like a feud within a family to which Olson did not belong.

Olson's opposition to New England white Anglo-Saxon Protestant culture ran very deep. When Matthiessen killed himself on April Fool's Day 1950, Olson responded with a poem, "Diaries of Death," in which Matthiessen's suicide is attributed to New England, "Inheritor of wrongs! of values which are useless." The only solution Olson saw for Matthiessen, surrounded by a culture in which he was, as a homosexual, as much an outcast as Olson was for his ancestry, would have been to escape, to "go free / from places where the strictures are too much, too much / for you and me to bear!" (*CP,* 144).

From 1941 to 1942, Olson worked for the Common Council for American Unity, a New York–based organization that fought the kind of ethnic and racial prejudice he had known in New England. In the autumn of 1942, he joined the Roosevelt administration as assistant chief of the Foreign Language Division of the Office of War Information, where his job was to make government policy presentable to various ethnic groups. (For example, he wrote a pamphlet called *Spanish Speaking Americans in the War.*) This position entailed considerable bureaucratic frustration, however, and Olson soon assumed a jaundiced view of the Washington political labyrinths. Frustrated in their own jobs, his superiors resigned, leaving him suddenly the likely choice for head of the division. Recognizing the difficulties he too might face, he resigned as well. By this time, however, Olson had established a strong reputation for himself as a specialist in ethnic matters, and he was soon appointed foreign nationalities director for the Democratic National Committee. Then Truman became president, and Olson abandoned a political future.

A few months later, Olson read Ernest Fenollosa's *The Chinese Written Character as a Medium for Poetry,* which was heavily indebted to New England transcendentalism in general and to Emerson in particular. Fenollosa's work was soon fundamental to Olson's poetics and one of the principal routes by which Emerson assumed a central role in his work.

Olson, as noted earlier, professed great disdain for Emerson, attacking him, for example, for "stupid transcendentalism the corpse cold universalism of brattle street." [11] Following Melville, Olson rejected all forms of idealism or

POETRY AS POLITICS

Platonism—all attempts, that is, to understand the cosmos in terms of absolutes—and the idealist Emerson became a particular target.

Emerson's metaphysics had been a problem for his successors from Whitman to William James and Gertrude Stein, but his concept of experience as process, as perpetual mutation, had repeatedly reemerged in American intellectual and imaginative life. Each of his heirs was left to devise his or her own explanation for the source of freedom that followed what was in effect a liberation from history. Whitman's explanation lay in sexuality and desire; Stein's in personality and language and its ability to generate meaning. Olson, following suggestions in Fenollosa's work, located the source in "energy" or "push," particularly as manifest in the kinetics of language. Philip Kuberski pointed out that energy was "Olson's Being, Presence, Spirit, a kind of poetic or metaphysical principle not very different from the kinds that circulate in the German Idealists"—and very much, one should add, like Emerson's Oversoul.[12]

But a debt to Emerson was clearly difficult for Olson to acknowledge; Melville had rejected Emerson and idealist philosophies generally, and Olson clearly saw himself in Melville's camp. Lecturing at the University of British Columbia in 1963, he remarked that Emerson and Thoreau were "misleading men" and that "Melville shot 'em down every time."[13] At Black Mountain College, there was a well-established "Index," according to his biographer Tom

CHARLES OLSON

Clark, of writers Olson thought best ignored, and Emerson was prominent among them.[14] Olson, Duncan recalled, could be "narrow-minded," "great on Melville, but Black Mountain students were *not* supposed to read Emerson"— a problem particularly for Duncan, who identified himself as "an Emerson person."[15]

In his "Notes on Poetics Regarding Olson's *Maximus*," Duncan pointed out that one found "foreshadowings or forelightings of *Maximus*" in Emerson, notably in Olson's "aesthetic based on energies."[16] Olson's debt was finally too strong to be denied, and at last, in his 1968 lectures at Beloit College, he identified the American transcendentalists as "our predecessors."[17]

Sherman Paul is one of the most perceptive commentators on Black Mountain poetics and the author of *Emerson's Angle of Vision,* one of the subtlest expositions of Emerson's thought yet published. In his book *Olson's Push* he points out various ways in which Olson belongs in the Emersonian tradition.[18] As a teacher and scholar as well as a "thinker-at-large," for example, he met Emerson's description of the American scholar; Emerson's phrase "university of knowledges" is an apt description of Olson's scholarly ambitions. More significant, Emerson's definition of a poem as a "meter-making argument," his notion that form and idea must be inseparable, is fundamental to Olson's "Projective Verse."

Olson's work, wrote Paul, "more than he realized . . . is continuous" with romanticism and transcendentalism.[19]

POETRY AS POLITICS

Olson was, according to Paul, indebted to Emerson for "the romantic element in American thought appreciated by Santayana: "the primacy of experience"—the same element that William James borrowed for his own pragmatic philosophy and that in turn found its way into the work of Gertrude Stein and later the work of Robert Creeley.[20]

But the principal route through which Emerson reached Olson was Fenollosa, who drew his notion of language as process in part from Emerson. A Harvard-educated native of Massachusetts, Fenollosa became an instructor in philosophy in Japan, where he studied Eastern languages. At his death he left both the notes and translations out of which Ezra Pound fashioned *Cathay* and the manuscript for *The Chinese Written Character as a Medium for Poetry,* which Pound published in 1920.

Although the subject of *The Chinese Written Character as a Medium for Poetry* is Eastern languages and literature, the viewpoint from which Fenollosa wrote was largely Emersonian; he looked at the East through a transcendentalist's eyes. "We need in poetry thousands of active words," he wrote, "each doing its utmost to show forth the motive and vital forces"[21]—a statement that would have considerable influence on Western poets, though it was substantively no more than Emerson had said when he argued that language, unless ossified in dictionaries, was process, "vehicular and transitive."[22] As Hugh Kenner pointed out, Emerson's notion that language was "fossil poetry" can be felt behind Fenollosa's statement that poetry "was once in the language itself, and still underlies the dry bones of even our dictionaries."[23]

Fenollosa also attacked "the inveterate logic of classification"—the transformation of experience into facts and categories: "We should beware of modern narrow utilitarian meanings ascribed to the words in commercial dictionaries," he wrote. Nature, he continued, was "a vast storehouse of forces," and language, when not constrained by logic and classification, articulated power. In nature, he said, a sentence was "a flash of lightning. It passes between two terms, a cloud and the earth." Truth could be defined as "the *transference* of *power*."[24] Or, as Olson would say in "Projective Verse," "a poem is energy transferred from where the poet got it . . . , by way of the poem itself to, all the way over to, the reader" (*HU,* 52).

The presence of Emerson and Fenollosa can be felt in "La Torre" (first drafted in 1946 but much revised before its publication in 1953), in which Olson rejects the decorous restraint and the respect for poetic tradition that characterize his earlier poetry. According to "La Torre," destruction is the beginning of new action, new power: "To destroy / is to start again . . . (*CP,* 189).

In "The Quaker Graveyard in Nantucket," which was also written at this time and was immediately accepted by critics as a major poem, Robert Lowell retreats into established poetic conventions and religious orthodoxy. Both poets were responding to World War II, but while Lowell

POETRY AS POLITICS

withdrew into a stable past, Olson celebrated inevitable change, even when it was violent. Of the two responses, Lowell's was closer to the national temper. The country was on the verge of what he would call "the tranquilized fifties," a decade of conformity and restraint in which the energy and anarchic freedom of Olson's poetics would be anomalies.

"The Kingfishers," written in 1949, is Olson's first major poem—the first fully realized instance of what he would soon call projective verse. It is divided into three parts, in each of which he deals with what seems at first miscellaneous information and facts. The first part, for example, involves a discussion at a party about the feathers of kingfishers, once used as a basis of trade; the *E* on the omphalus at Delphi; and Mao's revolution. The poem might be seen as a collage, an arrangement of contrasts and juxtapositions similar to that in Eliot's "The Waste Land," or as an attempt at Pound's ideogramic method. But while these are certainly among Olson's models, his poetics are more complex. Collage and the ideogramic method bring seemingly unrelated material into a new resolution, whereas Olson's intention is to keep oppositions in play; the energy they generate is Olson's objective.

"The Kingfishers" has been the subject of a number of intensive readings, the most useful of which include those by George Butterick and Burton Hatlen. Hatlen treated the poem "as a verbal action" rather than "a sequence of images or symbols which body forth a meaning that the poet wants to communicate." He noted the distinction Olson made between "art" and "discourse" and indicated Olson's own sense of the inadequacy of the latter in any discussion of the former. "Because acceptable academic critical discourse must be unified around a central point," Hatlen wrote, "critics are likely to regard as unimaginable (or, at least, intolerably confused) any text not so unified." [25]

The poem, said Hatlen, should be read as "a kinetic event." He pointed out, for example, that the opening line ("What does not change / is the will to change" [*CP,* 86]) moves from a position of rest and "being" in its first half into the kinesis and "becoming" of the second, out of which the poem then unfolds. In Olson's view, said Hatlen, the "poem that moves, that allows itself to be a kinetic force traveling through space-time, truly does escape the trap of meaning," which entails resolution rather than change.[26]

"The Kingfishers" establishes a field of tensions among its various points of reference. References to the kingfisher merge with references to the omphalos and with Mao's call for action to the Communist Party: "La lumière de l'aurore est devant nous, nous devons lever et agir." The *E* on the omphalos and the kingfisher, sacred bird of Mayan and Aztec cultures, return the imagination to the genesis of time and thought, and Mao's words remind the reader that beginnings, the new, are an eternal recurrence.

But whatever literal reading one constructs in trying to impose a conventional order on these lines, the poem's

POETRY AS POLITICS

effectiveness depends on the reader's seeing it as an energy field in which references like these react against and with each other. The poem is like thought itself in juggling numerous ideas simultaneously and in the leaps of attention that do not require logical explanation. It is in that juggling and the dexterity it requires, as opposed to whatever "meaning" can be extracted from the poem, that Olson's achievement is found.

"When the attentions change / the jungle leaps in," Olson wrote. "The Kingfishers" is intellectually syncopated, allowing new ideas, new observations to enter the poem at any point and shatter expectation. One principle underlying this is "feedback" ("the feed-back is the law" [*CP,* 89], Olson declares)—a term borrowed from the Harvard mathematician Norbert Wiener: memories from events that precede the poem merge with illuminative moments within it to further intensify the complex texture of references or field of intellectual energies. Through this combination the past is not neutralized but repeatedly reemerges to affect the present.

The poem obviously favors a reader who shares its range of references, and the best guide to that is George Butterick, who identified not only the "Fernand" mentioned in the opening lines of the poem but even the location of the party he is attending. According to Butterick, the poem offers "a narrator who, by determination of will and grasp of intellect, is equal to the events presented. He is not an imperious spokesman; in fact he is much less a narrator than a narrator imperative. Events tell themselves." In short, Olson moves beyond lyrical poetry, which arises from the personality of the speaker, into a poetry that takes its force from the complexity of its materials. The foundation is laid here, wrote Butterick, for *The Maximus Poems,* "without the hero Maximus and without the focus of Gloucester but with all the motive."[27]

Although "The Kingfishers" involves primarily a field of competing energies that resist resolution, there are obvious thematic centers. For one thing, the poem suggests the impermanence of civilizations yet points out that things that were once integral to them—the omphalos, the kingfishers' feathers—remain powerful in the imagination. The omphalos at Delphi, which the ancients took to be the center of the universe, had inscribed on it the letter *E*. What that letter meant has long been forgotten, yet it still has the power to provoke speculation. The feathers of the kingfisher once had monetary value, but now one speculates on why that changed—and on their beauty. An energy field of great complexity that has nothing to do with the current practicalities of economic and political life reveals itself in the convergence of a multiplicity of seemingly unrelated events and ideas, and that convergence is itself the poem. Contemporary economic and political life, Truman's America, is criticized as "pudor pejoracracy": "shall you uncover honey," Olson asks, "/ where maggots are?" (*CP,* 93) Then he adds, "I hunt among stones"—namely, the omphalos, the Aztec ruins, all those remains of the past which, because of their continued imaginative suggestiveness, provide materials from which poems can be built (*CP,* 93).

"Projective Verse," published in *Poetry New York* in 1950, outlined the poetics behind poems like "The Kingfishers." The essay was quickly recognized as a major statement for avant-garde poetics. William Carlos Williams excerpted sections of it in his autobiography, and it was crucial in defining the directions followed by poets as otherwise diverse as Allen Ginsberg, Michael McClure, and Jeremy Prynne.

In this essay, Olson opposed what he had done in "The Kingfishers" to "'closed verse,' that verse which print bred,"—the kind of poetry that had been written by Wordsworth and Milton, to use his examples, and that was currently being refined by Richard Wilbur and Robert Lowell (*HU,* 51). In place of verse dependent on traditional poetic forms, Olson stressed breath and sound as points where poems should begin. He wanted a poetry with the spontaneity and immediacy of speech rather than the reflection and intentionality of writing.

He argued that poetic structure should derive from the poet's physiological presence in the words. "The HEAD," he wrote, moved "by way of the EAR, to the SYLLABLE," so that the structure of the word indicated meaning; "the HEART," or feeling, moved "by way of the BREATH, to the LINE" (*HU,* 55). In his view, the line and the breath, rather than the head or the intellect, were the greater powers. This notion had long been common among expressionist writers like William Faulkner, William Saroyan, Thomas Wolfe, and Henry Miller. It can be traced in American literature back to Emerson, who argued in "Poetry and Imagination" that "the length of lines in songs and poems is determined by the inhalation and exhalation of the lungs."[28] Among Olson's contemporaries, shortly before "Projective Verse" was published, Muriel Rukeyser made a similar claim: the poetic line, she insisted, "is intimately bound with the poet's breathing."[29]

Like Olson, Rukeyser believed that "the work that a poem does is a transfer of human energy."[30] Another point argued by Olson, namely that "form is never more than the extension of content" (the wording, as he said in the essay, was Robert Creeley's), is essentially a restatement of conventional romantic organicism. William Saroyan had made a similar claim a decade earlier in his essay "American Qualities": "If a man says twenty words that are fresh and genuine, these words are themselves form."[31]

"Projective Verse" is a manifesto for a new poetry, but it is also a scholar's project, a compilation of notions about poetics that were not always new and that Olson repeatedly attributed to others, as if his own poetic practice were not sufficient authority in itself. He pointed to Edward Dahlberg, for example, as his source for the dictum "One perception

POETRY AS POLITICS

must immediately and directly lead to a further perception" (*HU,* 52).

The derivative and scholarly nature of much that Olson had to say led Marjorie Perloff to describe "Projective Verse" as little more than a rewriting of arguments Pound, Williams, Fenollosa, and others had formulated years earlier : "a scissors and paste job, a clever but confused collage."[32] Perloff was right in one sense: Olson was speaking in the essay as a derivative poet and thinker. But his statement contained major shifts in emphasis from the poetics of his immediate predecessors, such as Pound. Olson scrapped the modernist desire to salvage the Western cultural tradition and erected in its place a vision of poetry unaligned to any cultural or political expediency. What he had to say was often common practice, but he pushed his points with particular fervor.

Although "Projective Verse" is wrapped in a scholar's cloak, it has the force and conviction of an evangelist's sermon. The essay is, after all, more than a manifesto in poetics; it is Olson's declaration of independence, his announcement that, after years of struggle, he has proven himself justified in abandoning the academic and bureaucratic careers that might so easily have been his. His fundamental point in the essay was that in the end there is no authority, not even the authority of "Projective Verse."

The latter part of the essay makes clear how extreme Olson's libertarian and anarchistic position had become.

CHARLES OLSON

Here he proposed what he called "objectism," his name for what he would later call a "stance toward reality." Objectism entailed eliminating "the lyrical interference of the individual as ego" (*HU,* 59); after all the ego may be merely a social identity, a wall between whatever one truly is and the natural world. Olson wanted a return to the most primitive, unmediated sources of expression. The projective poet, he concluded, would go "down through the workings of his own throat to that place where ... all act springs" (*HU,* 61). Olson wanted art that did not merely discuss or order its subject but in some way actually embodied it. Given his sense of a universe in continual flux, that requirement meant he wanted poetry of a kind exemplified by "The Kingfishers," in which the elements were never wholly at rest: "Art does not seek to describe but to enact" (*HU,* 10).

Olson recognized a binary opposition between a poetry of definition and a poetry of process. The former, he believed, establishes hierarchies of signification, asserting relationships in a static Ptolemaic cosmos; movement in that kind of poetry exists in the process whereby a work moves toward definition, resolution, and closure. But in Olson's view, there would be no closure, and the only constant would be the work of art itself: "The structures of the real are flexible," he believed elsewhere; "quanta do dissolve into vibrations, all does flow, and yet is there, to be made permanent, if the means are equal" (*HU,* 122).

Centering "all act" within the self meant liberation from obligation to external authority, but it also meant that

POETRY AS POLITICS

there was nowhere to turn for deliverance from suffering. That recognition is at the heart of another early poem, "In Cold Hell, in Thicket":

> . . . but hell now
> is not exterior, is not to be got out of, is
> the coat of your own self, . . .
>
> (*CP,* 158)

Projective verse implied a new epistemology. If "all act" had its center and its point of initiation within the self, then any sense one had of oneself as a victim had to be reconsidered; the self could no longer be viewed as simply the object of forces outside itself.

The difficulty that Olson faced with respect to this point can be seen in his attempts to rethink what history was and to distinguish his own position from that of the two modernist poets to whom he was closest, Ezra Pound and William Carlos Williams. "The Kingfishers" responds both to the economics of the Roosevelt administration and to the completely different but equally schematic economics preached by Pound. Roosevelt and Pound saw individuals as victims of history and believed that economic problems could be altered through education and legislation. In "The Kingfishers," such solutions are themselves part of the problem: both involve aggression, the imposing of one person's will on another. The historical changes with which the poem is concerned—the collapse of the Mayan and Aztec cultures, the destruction of Delphic traditions by the Byzantines, Mao's revolution—are variously good or bad, but all entail suffering. The solution is in effect an escape from history and redemption through imagination: "I hunt among stones." The poem becomes the expression of the individual seeker.

Pound, however, had defined an epic as "a poem containing history,"[33] and his choice of the word *containing* is crucial, implying that history was separate from the poet, indeed complete, before it was brought into the poem. History, Pound believed, was an economic process, and its axis was currency, not language. Pound, as Michael Bernstein said, believed that the poet "merely arranges what is already there."[34] He wanted history itself to speak in the poem, although in fact his historical vision in the *Cantos* is very personal.

Pound's sense of history as a seemingly objective presence may have made it easier for him to pursue his anti-Semitic views, or at least to pursue them without assuming personal responsibility for them: anti-Semitism, he could think, was justified by the course of history. In "A Lustrum for You, E. P.," Olson addressed Pound in the conflicted tones of one who has learned from him but recognizes and takes issue with his profound anti-Semitism. The poem pictures Pound as a "lover of the obscene" and says that he is "undone" by it (*CP,* 39). At the same time that the poem was written, however, Olson defended Pound in an essay,

POETRY AS POLITICS

"This Is Yeats Speaking." Recognizing that Pound had been "false–out of phrase—when he subordinated his critical intelligence to the objects of authority in others," Olson argued that one whose *Cantos* "concerns itself so much with the men who made . . . [the] Revolution" deserved something other from his country than simply the charge of treason (*HU,* 100. 102). Though "A Lustrum for You, E. P." is blunt in its tone and judgments, it still portrays the poet as superior to his errors, however abhorrent. At the poem's end, Olson charges Pound to continue to be a maker, a craftsman, but he does so in a form that mixes respect with reproach. Borrowing a sentence Pound used in the *Cantos* ("Adamo me fecit"—Adam made me—a sentence he had found inscribed on a column in a church in Verona), Olson concludes by charging Pound to "fecit"—a rude bilingual pun that Pound could not have missed. As one would expect from Olson's earlier efforts to dislodge American racial and ethnic prejudice, he had only scorn and contempt for Pound's anti-Semitism. It had been prejudices of this sort that had led the Byzantines to destroy Delphi and the conquistadors to destroy the Mayan and Aztec cultures. Pound's persistent anti-Semitism even in the face of reports about the Holocaust eventually led to an irrevocable break between the two men.

Olson's "There Was a Youth Whose Name Was Thomas Granger" (1947) both borrows techniques from Pound and illustrates the moral ground that separated the two poets. The device of citing historical documents and allowing the citations to speak for themselves, a technique used often in *The Maximus Poems,* was one that Pound had developed in his Malatesta cantos. But while Pound's cantos celebrate a man who was one of the great villains of history, Olson used New England documents to show how inhumane the Puritans had been. Granger, executed for sodomy, appears in the poem, despite the arguments of the official record, as essentially the victim of intolerance asserted as high morality—the kind of intolerance, that is, of which Pound was guilty.

But how was one to overcome those who persecuted people like Granger? The answer is given in "Conqueror" (1948): "Revolution proceeds out of a man" (*CP,* 73). Olson's solution was to find a revolution that was not just another aggression, however "benevolent" its motivations. "The Kingfishers" portrays exactly the kind of revolution he intended; it expresses the view that there are no laws of human nature or economics; no grand processes like those posed by Darwin, Marx, and Freud; no divine authority—nothing that can be used to excuse history as a complex of abstract, impersonal forces. By asserting, with Heraclitus, "What does not change / is the will to change," "The Kingfishers" denies the very idea of natural "law" to which individuals are subject and which they can use to justify their actions. The individual, in the context of this poem, is the force at work in history, and it is with the individual that responsibility for suffering lies.

POETRY AS POLITICS

Williams's credo "No ideas but in things" was shared by Olson, who followed him in borrowing cadences and vocabulary from ordinary speech, but a stronger tie between the two poets is evident in poems like "Lower Field—Enniscorthy" (1945) in its precise rendering of the literal landscape. Like Williams, Olson reserved his respect for the matter-of-fact rather than the visionary. He took a Williams-like pragmatic stance in "The Praises," in which he asked "that the work get done, and quickly / without the loss of due and profound respect for / the materials" (*CP,* 100).

In the late 1920s, Williams assembled notes for a meditative and critical book, *The Embodiment of Knowledge,* which was to be among other things a critique of intellectual life shaped by theories and facts. "Poetry," said Williams, "is all of a piece, knowledge presented in the form of pure writing which is made of the writing itself." He knew that readers would look for "sense" in Pound but advised that one should "[read] the verse," thus "entering . . . the actual field of the subject." Science and philosophy offered nothing but sense, he said, and promoted an idealized, abstract, and inhuman realm of absolute truth. For Williams, the solution to the trap of intellectuality was sensual experience. "Rely on the direct observation of the senses," he counseled; "Judge by the eyes and ears, touch and taste—reject everything from no matter what source that is without a place there." An individual was determined by his or her point in history, Williams believed, and the individual's experience, rather than abstract analysis and classification, should be where knowledge begins.[35]

Williams sounds very much like Olson here, and Olson may have learned from Williams, but he did not ultimately find the older man's work itself satisfactory. Williams's rejection of any "truth" that did not arise from direct experience kept him from the pure antiquarianism that a regionalist might have valued, but he was still, Olson believed, locked in nostalgia for an earlier "blueberry America" in spite of "Jersey dumpsmoke covering same."[36] He had a subject—"blueberry America"—that existed in memory only and could be sentimental. But Pound's "Yurrup" was equally irretrievable. Olson wanted to find a version of history that was as immediate as his everyday world—a history that would not be sentimental or influenced by the European heritage of classical civilization, a tradition he thoroughly rejected. It would be a history rooted in the New World, celebrating Mayans rather than Greeks, Aztecs rather than Romans.

The American groundwork for Olson's strategy is explicit in "To Gerhardt, There, Among Europe's Things of Which He Has Written Us in His 'Brief an Creeley und Olson' " (1951). The poet Rainer Maria Gerhardt was one of the first Europeans poets to adopt projectivist poetics. In his poem, translated for *Origin* as "Letter for Creeley and Olson," Gerhardt agreed that the Greeks had been the source of the failings of Western civilization—a powerful

POETRY AS POLITICS

admission for a German, whose culture had, long before Goethe, provided one of the principal means through which Greek thought was transmitted to the West. But Olson wanted that tradition dismissed; it was not enough to recognize the source of the problem: "Come here" he insisted to Gerhardt, "where we will welcome you / with nothing but what is" (*CP,* 219).

Sherman Paul has argued that history serves in Olson's work the function that nature serves in Emerson's: history is the master narrative, the great resource, not in Pound's sense of something external to the ego to be appropriated and "contained" in the poem but rather as a fundamental shaping power for the poem and fiber in its construction.[37] Nature, for Emerson, was poetry's source, and just as he removed nature from the hands of biologists and redefined it in moral and metaphysical terms, so Olson reconceived history as a force very different from the way it had been variously seen since Thucydides.

Emerson too had tried to reconceive history as something other than the record of political and economic forces, and there are substantial similarities between his view and Olson's. In his essay "History," he took the individual as an "incarnation" of "the universal mind," its "only and sovereign agent," and reasoned that "universal mind" made itself known to the individual as laws, which were then made manifest in facts: "all the facts of history preëxist in the mind as laws." The individual was not, therefore, shaped by history; history was the expression of what the individual fundamentally was: an incarnation of the universal mind. "All history becomes subjective," Emerson concluded; "there is properly no history; only biography."[38]

Olson rethought history in similar ways, but in his view its ultimate source was not a Platonic universal mind but eros. "Human Universe" is one of Olson's principal attempts to understand history in a way that would not contradict his profoundly subjective poetics. The essay is in part the product of his contact with Mayan culture, which he believed had been much less warlike and aggressive, or "Roman," than is now known to have been the case. What he imagined was a nonviolent people living in an intense and immediate relationship to their physical world. The Maya that Olson imagined—"moving their heads so nervously to stay alive, to keep alerted to what they were surrounded by" (*HU*, 12)—are idealizations of what he believed poets should be, finding "no ideas but in things."

Olson's version of Mayan culture may also have been shaped by D. H. Lawrence's fanciful reconstruction of the Etruscans. According to Tom Clark, Olson read Lawrence's *Etruscan Places* in the winter of 1945, shortly before reading Fenollosa, and took particular note of Lawrence's characterization of the Etruscan priest as one for whom "the blood was the red stream of consciousness itself." Olson's essay "The Escaped Cock: Notes on Lawrence & the Real" concerns Lawrence's pursuit of this "truth." One should

POETRY AS POLITICS

struggle to feel the world fully in his or her blood: as he said in "Human Universe," the Maya had been "hot for the world they lived in, . . . hot to get it down the way it was" (*HU,* 15).

How did one that lay at the core of Olson's argument with the Greeks and with traditional views of history. What he needed was a Copernican revolution—a completely new way of viewing the past that would allow it to be seen as something other than an inevitable process, for if its process was self-generating or inevitable, one could never escape from the Greeks.

Olson's first major attempt to rethink the concept of history occurs in "History," an essay he sent to Creeley for comment in 1952. Taking as his first (and unexamined) principal that "all events are only our own actions," Olson was able to argue that there was no master plan (economic laws, for example) beyond the self.[39] But what then were the stories called "history"? In *The Art of the Logos,* Olson noted, J. A. K. Thomson had shown that *logos* originally meant "what is said"—the same thing that Homer meant by *muthos.* The words were interchangeable. When Stesichorus said that the logos in a particular episode in Homer was false, he meant only that it had factual errors; the story itself was still true. Pindar, however, distinguished between muthos and logos, as did Plato and the philosophic tradition that began with him. For them, logos was now distinct from *myth* or *story*—now considered the particular property of poets. Herodotus, on the other hand, had retained the older definition; he set out to find not "truth" but "evidence."

"Each of us," Olson insisted, "is the only imaginable fact & 'truth' there could or can ever be." The philosopher's ideal of abstract, general truths separate from those who thought them was a dangerous illusion, he believed. Logos existed only in and through the individual, and like Herodotus, one should go in search of the "evidence" with which to tell one's own story. Thucydides had made history a continuum of facts in what seemed objectively to be patterns of cause and effect. The focus had shifted from the "act" of storytelling in Herodotus to the "facts" of the story in Thucydides. Similarly, the Greeks replaced art (the individual expression of muthos) with culture (the repetition of predicable aesthetic patterns). The direct result of shifts like this, said Olson, taking his words from Heraclitus, was that "man is estranged from that with which he is most familiar, and he must continuously seek to rediscover it." [40]

With this as his basic argument, Olson elaborated over the next four years the notions that coalesced in the series of lectures he delivered at Black Mountain in 1956 and that were published fourteen years later as *The Special View of History.* Alfred North Whitehead's *Process and Reality,* which Olson first read in 1955, was particularly valuable to him in this work, providing a closely reasoned, Aristotelian argument for viewing the universe as perpetual process. Whitehead, an admirer of Emerson, saw "the World" as

POETRY AS POLITICS

"primordially many, namely, the many actual occasions with their physical finitude" but understood that "in the process it acquires a consequent unity, which is a novel occasion and is absorbed into the multiplicity of the primordial character."[41] Here was an argument that led to conclusions very much like those Olson had been insisting on in his own work. "Whitehead," he said near the beginning of the first of his lectures in this series, "has written the metaphysic of the reality we have acquired."[42] He had become, Olson later said, "my great master and the companion of my poem [*The Maximus Poems*]."[43]

The Special View of History opens with Heraclitus' aphorism that man is now estranged from that with which he is most familiar—followed by Keats's definition of "Negative Capability" as that state "when man is capable of being in uncertainties, Mysteries, doubts, without any irritable reaching after fact & reason" (*SVH,* 14). Keats, as Olson realized it, provided a solution to the predicament Heraclitus had identified: if one could stop reaching for answers as the Greeks had led civilization to do, one would be able to repossess the self.

The West, said Olson, was a victim of the shift in Athenian culture during the fifth century B.C.E. to philosophy, classification ("mere taxonomy," he wrote elsewhere), and logic ("sticks in a stiff box") (*HU,* 119). From that point, civilization had entered a humanistic era that had since dissolved. A period without definition or force had followed (a "void," he said), but now civilization was entering a new humanistic era, one that would not be shackled with the legacies of Socrates and Greek philosophy, analytical reason and classification. The new humanism would be marked by will, force, energy—the world would be essentially Nietzschean. The individual would be driven by will to create and become the center of history rather than its victim: "Will is the foundation of our speech," Olson concluded; "we catch the demiurge in the act" (*SVH,* 32).

For Emerson, history was the result of cosmic laws that were revealed through the self; but Olson, like Nietzsche, saw it as directly the "function" of the self (*SVH,* 17). Olson's problem at this point was to avoid the obvious charge that all history was, therefore, solipsistic. He found the solution in Carl Gustav Jung, whose work he had recently been reading with excitement. In Jung's notion of the collective unconscious lay a modern surrogate for Emerson's Oversoul and a way of seeing history as more than an individual's solipsistic fantasy. History could now be understood as the experience of the group as revealed through the individual, a notion that would be crucial to *The Maximus Poems;* in the bedrock of the collective unconscious, self and community were one.

Olson believed that he had found "the new localism, a polis" that would take the place of the one that had eroded since Pindar and Plato (*SVH,* 25). If anyone felt that his

POETRY AS POLITICS

concept of this polis implied disorder or anarchy (not an unreasonable supposition, as Olson did not seem to be interested in government and legal controls), he added, for whatever consolation it might provide, that chaos in a truly natural state was nothing but "multiplicity" (*SVH,* 51). All things were ultimately related; the woes of history were in large part the result of thinking that only certain kinds of abstract ordering were acceptable.

What he was teaching, Olson concluded, was "stance toward reality" (*SVH,* 36), but this stance was clearly male; *The Special View of History* is Olson's fullest attempt to justify a return to what he had once called "the primordial & phallic energies & methodologies" (*HU,* 23). Robert O'Brien Hokanson argued that Olson, in his own scale of values, "'projects' most 'like a man' when he attempts to assert his identity and authority, when he presents his ideals and his solutions to what ails poetry and the world." [44] The sexism implicit in Olson's poetics here obviously compromises his vision; his brave new world is essentially a world for men. It is odd that one whose political career had been so committed to eradicating racial, ethnic, and religious prejudice should have been so blind.

Olson's poetry is available now largely because of the efforts of George Butterick. During his final years, Olson supported himself principally through teaching appointments, lectures, and readings. As he moved from place to place, his manuscripts accumulated, and after his death, it was principally Butterick who transcribed and ordered them. He selected from manuscripts, published poems, and variant versions the works in *The Collected Poems* (1987). (He also edited a second volume, *A Nation of Nothing but Poetry* [1989], which includes poems and variants he had rejected for *The Collected Poems*). His work was extremely important to the publication of the third volume of *The Maximus Poems;* Olson died in 1970 before he was able to gather the poems for this volume into a sequence. Butterick, with the help of Olson's literary executor at the time, Charles Boer, selected and ordered the poems for the third volume and expanded it somewhat on his own when he prepared the complete edition. This would have been a major task in any event, but it was made more so by the fact that *The Maximus Poems* is not to be read as a series of related works—like Duncan's *The Opening of the Field,* for example—but as a coherent sequence, a single grand poem like Williams's *Paterson.*

The Maximus Poems begins as didactic letters from Maximus to the people of Gloucester. The didactic voice becomes less common as the work proceeds, however; it is more the voice of one who has learned how "to loose [itself] in time and space," circling out to include subjects from economics to myth, boyhood memories to Puritan history. Superficially, Maximus was modeled on a neo-Platonist philosopher, Maximus of Tyre, and it may seem odd that

POETRY AS POLITICS

Olson would have been attracted to a Platonist, but the preface to the edition of Maximus that he read, Butterick pointed out, also described the philosopher as a sophist, a student of rhetoric, "placing the end of life in *practical* and not in *theoretic* virtue."[45] Butterick noted that, at a reading in 1962, Olson admitted to having little interest in the historical Maximus, but he valued him for other reasons: Maximus had traveled throughout the Mediterranean and was a focus of interest wherever he went; he was his own Delphi, his own "navel of the world." "We come from a whole line of life that makes Delphi that center," Olson argued, ". . . and this I think is the kind of thing that ought to be at least disturbed."[46] The center of the world could as easily be Tyre as Delphi; that determination depended on the individual, not tradition, history, politics, or culture.

Olson's point is suggested by the first and last lines in the final volume—the only sections that he insisted had to be included and placed where they are. The opening lines, in their entirety, are as follows:

> having descried the nation
> to write a Republic
> in gloom on Watch-House Point[.]
>
> (*MP*, 377)

Watch-House Point is an old name for the part of Gloucester where Olson lived. *Maximus* proposed a repub-

CHARLES OLSON

lic, at least within the terms of *The Special View of History*. These lines were written eight years after those lectures, by which time Olson may have realized that his proposal, however feasible it may have seemed in the isolation of Black Mountain, had little chance of being realized, and that in turn may be the reason for the *gloom* in this first poem. The last line in the book is the list noted earlier of four personal things (the speaker's wife, car, color, and self), bringing the volume around full circle; for in Olson's thought, of course, the Republic and the self are the same.

Olson's idealized Gloucester, his polis, is really a self-sufficient nineteenth-century New England town, and in choosing that model he had, as in so many other ways, been anticipated by Emerson. As Richard Hutson demonstrated, Olson's Gloucester and Emerson's Concord are remarkably similar towns. Hutson pointed to the utopianism in Emerson's "critique of reform and of America in general," in which "all forms of organization, contracts, and associations" seem adversaries. "Despite [Emerson's] spiritual affirmations," wrote Hutson, "his advice is either passivity or complete dissolution of the political or civil or religious institutions of his time—except for the one institution that he depends upon, the New England town." Choosing not to live in Boston or Cambridge, as would have been expected of a New England intellectual, he settled in Concord, primarily at that time a farming village, which Emerson associated with the small, self-sufficient communities of

POETRY AS POLITICS

New England's past. Changes in the national economy—particularly with the coming of the railroad—soon forced changes in the town, but Emerson saw them as superficial; beneath the surface, he felt, things remained essentially the same. An individual's roots were moral and cosmic; one was an agent in a drama far beyond the control of bankers and entrepreneurs. As Hutson concluded, Emerson "translates the dying innocence of the New England town into his notion of a self that is at once individual and representative." [47]

Emerson's idealization of the New England town, Hutson pointed out, "anticipates the cultivation of the local in . . . Charles Olson." [48] Confronted with political and economic threats no less colossal in his own day than the railroad had been in Emerson's, Olson turned to the relatively isolated community of Gloucester—situated on an island—as the setting for his ideal polis. The town had always been dependent on fishing rather than manufacturing or trade for its economic base, but this was changing, and, like Emerson, Olson argued that the real core of the community was the individual; the individual in turn was free, or at least potentially free, of an invasive national culture threatening nuclear war and corporate control of the economy.

Olson's ideal community is a collection of individuals: "polis is / eyes" (*MP,* 30). In Olson's Gloucester, there are "no hierarchies, no infinite, no such many as mass, . . . only eyes in all heads, / to be looked out of" (*MP,* 33). Each citizen, like Herodotus, is left to construct his or her story: "looking / for oneself for the evidence of / what is said" (*MP,* 104–105). And there is no cause for Thoreauvian withdrawal, no isolation. "I believe in society," Olson said, "as religious" (*MP,* 422).

Politically, *The Maximus Poems* should be understood in terms of projects like Matthiessen's American civilization program at Harvard. Olson chose for his subject, after all, a town settled by Puritans but appropriated by Portuguese fishermen. Gloucester survived because of the very kind of people its older families scorned. On the first page of the book, Antony of Padua, patron saint of the Portuguese fishermen, is called upon to bless Gloucester. A few lines later there is a reference not to a white Congregational church such as one would expect in a small New England town but to the Church of Our Lady of Good Voyage. Those who had experienced the anti-Catholicism that pervaded New England in Olson's youth could not miss the point: the self-reliant Puritan settlers (to whom Olson returns in documents and accounts of Gloucester's past) had lost their world to people more worthy of the heritage, and it is these newcomers who must now resist economic exploitation.

One of the most effective, and often reprinted, poems in the collection is "Maximus to Gloucester, Letter 27 [withheld]," which opens with evocations of Gloucester as

POETRY AS POLITICS

Olson knew it in his boyhood. These reminiscences are broken suddenly with the assertion "This, is no bare incoming / of novel abstract form"—no storytelling, that is, of the kind that would have interested academic critics seeking out its formal conditions. Nor, Olson continued, is what he has said a "welter" of remembered things. Rather it is the "imposing" in language of what he has been and is. Gloucester has been transformed in this act of storytelling as much as Olson, or Maximus, has been transformed in passing from the childhood of his memories to the speaker he now is. Gloucester exists now within him and his speech: "Polis," he concludes, "is this" (*MP,* 184–85).

Olson resisted any effort to define community in terms of economics. But while Black Mountain was closing its doors, President Eisenhower approved the interstate highway system; and the year the first volume of *The Maximus Poems* was published, he warned the country against the "military-industrial complex." Olson knew that the country was headed toward a culture very different from the one he proposed in his polis. Nothing, on the other hand, was to be gained from nostalgically imagining a return to "blueberry America."

Nonetheless, Olson believed that his work could have political consequences. Speaking at the 1965 Berkeley Poetry Conference, he told an audience made up largely of poets, "If you don't know, brother, that poetics is politics, poets are political leaders today, and the only ones, you shouldn't have come."⁴⁹ Jack Spicer's sardonic response was a lecture pointing out that poetry had never had a practical effect on politics and that anyone who thought the situation would change was deluded. Spicer was correct, of course. *The Maximus Poems* had not done and would never do anything to stem the tide of corporate capitalism. If seacoast towns like Gloucester tried to prevent development, it was perhaps because the older buildings were better for the tourist trade.

The mocking tone that Olson used as a device to point out that America had become saturated with "mu-sick" and "Tell-A-Vision" (*MP,* 75) would never in itself change anything. He had in one sense become the kind of gadfly who assaults local newspapers with a blitz of letters to the editor (which is exactly what he did). A community like Black Mountain, idyllic in its isolation, or Gloucester as he remembered it from his boyhood, had vecome a museum or memory.

However reactionary Olson was politically, at least in the sense of advocating a return to the individualism of an earlier generation, he never echoed established poetics. In place, for example, of conventional lineation such as Shakespeare's "Th' expense of spirit in a waste of shame / Is lust in action," in which the line is broken between the subject and verb, Olson experimented with divisions like the following:

POETRY AS POLITICS

> love is form, and cannot be without
> important substance (the weight
> say, 58 carats each one of us, perforce
> our goldsmith's scale[.]
>
> (*MP*, 5)[50]

Another poet might have broken the lines after "form," "be," "substance," "say," and "us," or in some other way that would have reflected conventional syntactic and semantic divisions. But Olson's lines bring together associations and rhythmic divisions that are less obvious and, perhaps for this reason, more interesting. Thus "love" and "cannot be without" come together in one line, and "important substance" and "weight" appear in another, while the lines move through a series of steps through which love, first conceived of as form (a Platonic abstraction) becomes something understood as wholly physical, to be weighed in "the goldsmith's scale."

Avoiding the kind of resolution, definition, or closure preordained in conventional syntax, Olson often initiates a syntactical pattern without completing it (for example, by opening a parenthesis without closing it) or begins a sentence only to shift suddenly to a new rhythm or observation. In "Maximus to Gloucester, Letter 27 [withheld]," his reminiscences breaks off in mid-sentence "... under one of those frame hats women then") to be replaced immediately by a comment on the nature of the reminiscences themselves ("This, is no bare incoming / of novel abstract form . . ." [*MP,* 184]).

In violating syntactical and semantic expectations, Olson was able to make a sentence exactly what he wanted: a "capable animal . . . jumping all over the place"(*HU,* 65). He could be as aphoristic as Emerson or Nietzsche but then undercut the sense of closure and definition that aphorisms impart, by simply omitting a period—as he does in quoting Heraclitus at the opening of "The Kingfishers": "What does not change / is the will to change" (*CP,* 86). Conventional punctuation is often omitted in *Maximus*—including the last poem, which has no period, implying that the poem is always as open to new possibility as it was when it began.

Feedback also undercut closure, for things were not necessarily "finished"; they could reenter the system at any point. Documents from Puritan history, Olson's memories of childhood summers in Gloucester, bits and pieces from conversations and letters could enter the poem and set into play issues and ideas that had seemed resolved. Rather than submit to history as an inviolable integrity of cause and effect, the poet was free to roam through time as if it were space, which, as Olson argued in *Call Me Ishmael,* is what Melville had done with his "way of reaching back through time until he got history pushed back so far he turned time into space" (*CMI,* 14).

The notion of time as space, and the poem as a "field" of action rather than a sequential ordering of materials, allowed Olson the freedom to move, as Melville had done

POETRY AS POLITICS

in *Moby-Dick,* with great freedom and rapidity from one preoccupation to another, thereby suggesting what Whitehead called "the multiplicity of the primordial character." Particularly in the second and third volumes of *The Maximus Poems,* Olson was willing to move quickly and dexterously from one concern to another, confident that all were part of one vision and that if the connections were not immediately evident, they would eventually reveal themselves.

Olson has never been a canonical figure in the academy, but among the American avant-garde his work continues to be either a critical resource (as in the work of poets as otherwise various as Nathaniel Mackey, Gustaf Sobin, and Susan Howe) or the very thing to be criticized and resisted—particularly among such language poets as Barrett Watten and, because of his profound sexism, among some feminist poets. But whether Olson is seen as a poet to learn from or one to condemn, his work has a monumentality of intention that cannot be easily dismissed.

One of the principal impediments to evaluating Olson is a voice one finds here and there in both essays and poems. It is the voice of an individual lecturing his readers the way a professor lectures a seminar. "Discourse is such a lie," Olson wrote in "Letter for Melville 1951" (*CP,* 239), yet discourse is exactly what one finds repeatedly in his work. He attacked Duncan for pursuing "Wisdom as Such," but wisdom is what Maximus and *The Special View of History* purvey.

CHARLES OLSON

Olson was in some ways always the academic he condemned—a systematizer who believed in the individual as the only authority but who was always adding new experts to bolster his arguments. Utterly pedantic in matters of Melville incunabula, he could vault from physics to anthropology to mathematics with bewildering speed looking for evidence to support his poetics and his nineteenth-century libertarian politics. He did not hesitate to declare himself a student of Mayan culture, although he had little sense of how a field archeologist organizes evidence, with the result that his view of the Maya was largely a charming fiction.

The problem lay in his method. It was one thing to see logic and classification as too binding, but it was something quite different to ignore them because they overrode the vision he wanted to embrace. If, however, he had compromised and had reasoned his arguments more carefully, he might never have become that titanic Nietzschean presence—repudiating causality and conformity—who demonstrated throughout his own work that an individual could indeed will his or her own world into being. As a result, few innovative poets of his generation were and are heard with as much intensity by their peers; even fewer articulated as radical a transformation in poetics. One simply cannot understand the developments of the innovative tradition in American poetry without encountering the poems and poetics of Charles Olson.

POETRY AS POLITICS

Notes

1. F. O. Matthiessen, *American Renaissance: Art and Expression in the Age of Emerson and Whitman* (New York: Oxford University Press, 1941) 209, 415, 457–58.

2. Donald M. Allen, *The New American Poetry* (New York: Grove, 1960).

3. Charles Olson, *Call Me Ishmael: A Study of Melville* (New York: Reynal and Hitchcock, 1947) 13. Further references will be noted parenthetically in the text as *CMI*.

4. Olson, *The Collected Poems* (Berkeley: University of California Press, 1987) 6. Further references will be noted parenthetically in the text as *CP*.

5. Olson, *The Maximus Poems* (Berkeley and Los Angeles: University of California Press, 1983) 635. Further references will be noted parenthetically in the text as *MP*.

6. Merton M. Sealts, "Olson, Melville, and the New Republic," *Contemporary Literature* 22 (Spring 1981): 176.

7. Michael Bernstein, *The Tale of the Tribe* (Princeton: Princeton University Press, 1980) 241.

8. Quoted in Ezra Pound, *Selected Prose: 1909–1965* (London: Faber and Faber, 1973) 118.

9. Olson, *Human Universe and Other Essays* (New York: Grove, 1967) 117. Further references will be noted parenthetically in the text as *HU*.

10. Matthiessen, xv.

11. Olson and Robert Creeley, *The Complete Correspondence,* vol. 4, ed. George Butterick (Santa Barbara, Calif.: Black Sparrow Press, 1982) 41.

12. Philip Kuberski, "Charles Olson and the American

CHARLES OLSON

Thing: The Ideology of Literary Revolution," *Criticism: A Quarterly for Literature and the Arts* 27 (Spring 1985): 182.

13. Clark Coolidge, "Notes Taken in Classes Conducted by Charles Olson at the University of British Columbia, Vancouver, August 1963," *Olson* 4 (Fall 1975): 55.

14. Tom Clark, *Charles Olson: The Allegory of a Poet's Life* (New York: Norton, 1991) 209.

15. Quoted in Allen Ginsberg, *Allen Verbatim: Lectures on Poetry, Politics, Consciousness,* ed. Gordon Ball (New York: McGraw-Hill, 1974) 135.

16. Robert Duncan, *Fictive Certainties* (New York: New Directions, 1985) 68.

17. Olson, *Poetry and Truth: The Beloit Lectures and Poems,* ed. George F. Butterick (San Francisco: Four Seasons, 1971) 55. See also Sherman Paul's discussion of Emerson's value for Olson in *Olson's Push* (Baton Rouge and London: Louisiana State University Press, 1978) 273. My sense of Olson's debt to Emerson owes much to Paul, the foremost authority on the Emersonian tradition in America.

18. Paul, 273.

19. Paul, 102.

20. Paul, 49.

21. Ernest Fenollosa, *The Chinese Written Character as a Medium for Poetry, The Poetics of the New American Poetry,* ed. Donald Allen and Warren Tallman (New York: Grove, 1973) 31.

22. Ralph Waldo Emerson, *Essays: Second Series* (Boston and New Houghton, Mifflin, 1883) 37.

23. Hugh Kenner, *The Pound Era* (Berkeley and Los Angeles: University of California Press, 1971) 105.

POETRY AS POLITICS

24. Fenollosa, 18, 30, 31.

25. Burton Hatlen, "Kinesis and Meaning: Charles Olson's 'The Kingfishers' and the Critics," *Contemporary Literature* 30 (Winter 1989): 546, 551–52.

26. Hatlen, 570.

27. George Butterick, "Charles Olson's 'The Kingfishers and the Poetics of Change," *American Poetry* 6 (Winter 1989): 49.

28. Emerson, *Letters and Social Aims* (Boston and New York: Houghton, Mifflin, 1883) 49.

29. Muriel Rukeyser, *The Life of Poetry* (New York: 1948) 123.

30. Rukeyser, 185.

31. William Saroyan, "American Qualities," in J. Calder Joseph, *Narration with a Red Piano* (Cincinnati: Little Mann Press, 1940) 47.

32. Marjorie Perloff, "Charles Olson and the 'Inferior Predecessors' " *ELH* 40 (1973): 295.

33. Ezra Pound, *Literary Essays,* ed. T. S. Eliot (New York: New Directions, 1968) 86.

34. Bernstein, 39.

35. William Carlos Williams, *The Embodiment of Knowledge* (New York: New Directions, 1974) 73, 85, 135.

36. Olson and Creeley, *The Complete Correspondence,* vol. 5, ed. George F. Butterick (Santa Barbara, Calif.: Black Sparrow Press, 1983) 51.

37. Paul, 103.

38. Emerson, *Essays: First Series* (Boston and New York: Houghton, Mifflin, 1883) 9.

39. Olson and Creeley, *The Complete Correspondence,* vol. 9, ed. George F. Butterick (Santa Rosa, Calif.: Black Sparrow Press, 1989) 109.

40. Olson and Creeley, vol. 9, 9, 102, 121.

41. Alfred North Whitehead, *Process and Reality* (New York: Free Press, 1978) 349.

42. Olson, *The Special View of History,* ed. Ann Charters (Berkeley: Oyez, 1970) 16. Further references will be noted parenthetically in the text as *SVH*.

43. Olson, *Muthologos: The Collected Lectures and Interviews,* vol. 1, ed. George F. Butterick (Bolinas, Calif.: Four Seasons Foundation, 1978) 186.

44. Robert O'Brien Hokanson, "'Projecting' Like a Man: Charles Olson and the Poetics of Gender," *Sagetrieb* 9 (Spring/Fall 1990): 181.

45. Butterick, *A Guide to the Maximus Poems of Charles Olson* (Berkeley and Los Angeles: University of California Press, 1980) 6.

46. Butterick, *A Guide,* 7.

47. Richard Hutson, "Two Gardens: Emerson's Philosophy of History," in *The Green American Tradition: Essays and Poems for Sherman Paul,* ed. H. Daniel Peck (Baton Rouge and London: Louisiana State University Press, 1989) 32, 35.

48. Hutson, 38.

49. Clark, 325.

50. According to Butterick, Olson's choice of "58" was "arbitrary"; he originally had "50." In any case, the number "[lends] specificity . . . to the suggestion that each one is, or has within, the necessary measure of his own condition" (Butterick, *A Guide,* 11).

CHAPTER THREE

Robert Creeley:
Poetics of Solitude

All that would matter to me, finally, as a writer, is that the scale and the place of our common living be recognized, that the mundane in that simple emphasis be acknowledged.
—**Robert Creeley,** *Autobiography*

Being shy as a young man, I was very formal, and still am. I make my moves fast but very self-consciously.
—**Creeley,** *The Collected Essays*

In his review of *The Collected Poems of Robert Creeley, 1945–1975,* the poet Robert Hass reported having heard that when Creeley was an undergraduate at Harvard, he came to the conclusion that William Carlos Williams end-stopped his lines and, admiring Williams, began writing his own poems that way. The story, Hass thought, was probably not true (although it had "a wonderful rightness"); but several years later, Creeley admitted that in fact this was what had happened.[1]

If the lines in the following passage from Williams's "The Lily" were end-stopped, the words *of, window,* and *air* would receive special emphasis—much great emphasis than in conventional speech:

ROBERT CREELEY

> The branching head of
> tiger-lilies through the window
> in the air—[.] [2]

Hass pointed out that breaks like the one between the first and second lines were probably intended to speed the poem. Creeley's reading, on the other hand, gave lines of this sort a syncopated rhythm and "[threw] an odd emphasis on the last word in the line." Reading this way, said Hass, made "visible . . . the strangeness of the struggle to articulate the fact of the sentence." [3]

End-stopping the line also brought attention to prepositions, conjunctions, and articles—words that tend to slip by while the ear listens for "meaning." As Juan Amador Bedford pointed out in his study of Williams's influence on Creeley, Creeley's enjambment emphasizes the "thingness" of the terminal words, "underlines [their] integrity . . . and loads them with that energy that makes them reach forward toward the next line, thus stressing their importance and singularity." [4] At the same time, the technique suggests the arbitrary nature of syntax; broken in the middle, phrases lose the impression of inevitability that conventional grammatical structures and speech rhythms provide. Language reveals its artificial nature, and the artificiality of the way in which we make sense of the world is exposed.

For example, the statement "You are always with me, there is never a separate place" may at first sound as if it

POETICS OF SOLITUDE

could have been taken from any number of contexts in popular literature—a popular romance, for example, or a screenplay. An actor might deliver the line as if it were sentimental, but it takes on a very different force when it is arranged in end-stopped manner as in the following lines from Creeley's "Words":

> You are always
> with me,
> there is never
> a separate
>
> place.[5]

The hesitations and syncopations prompted by the sharp breaks at the ends of the lines enforce a rhythmic tension that is not otherwise apparent. In Hass's words, the reader is confronted with "the strangeness of the struggle to articulate the fact of the sentence."[6] The language has been fragmented in such a way that the ordinary is seen again for the ways in which it works. The reader sees again within the words an intention that had been lost and sentimentalized through overuse.

Creeley's lineation brings attention to the words as such, reminding the reader that it is ultimately words, as much as the speaker, that determine the limits of what can be said. As a writer, a person can be no more than his or her words; as Charles Bernstein said, "Writing becomes not the wish to express a self egocentrically but rather to hear—attend—the order of syllables in the world and in so sounding find who 'I' as a 'self' am."[7]

But whatever Creeley's method teaches about ways in which language permits certain possibilities and not others, it more importantly creates a distinctive and supple music. Creeley noted that his misreading of Williams led him to use line endings as "a way to ground and/or to locate a rhythmic base"; they were "pivots."[8] He was in this way able to create wholly new rhythmic patterns with the language—"the one genuinely original verbal music in the English language in the second half of the twentieth century," according to Hass.[9]

It is also a music very different from what one finds in any of Creeley's contemporaries, most obviously those endorsed by critics during his early career. These contemporaries were in a sense Creeley's opposition, for as long as their attentive reworkings of conventional prosody were what the universities and literary journals wanted, he was cut off from much of his possible audience.

Perhaps the most widely admired American poet at the time was Robert Frost, whose poetics provide an instructive contrast to Creeley's. Frost grounded his poems in "the sound of sense,"[10] taking from the spoken language tones and cadences that seemed meaningful in themselves; one didn't have to hear the actual words, that is, in order to understand and be affected by the literal argument of the

POETICS OF SOLITUDE

words. The idea that sense and the sound of sense are very different things can be disturbing, but it is the first principle of rhetoric: whether an argument is logical or honest, it can be made convincing if it is expressed in a certain way. In a poem, the sound of sense can be very seductive, but it can also be in some ways rhetorical and calculated—a poetic sleight of hand.

Frost's prosody is one instance of critical taste at midcentury, when calculation and mastery of conventional technique were much admired. The ideal was "the well-wrought urn," a complex, sophisticated structure that concealed the way in which the poem worked. Creeley's work challenged that tradition by placing the mechanics of the poem in the foreground. He confronted his reader not with the sound of sense but with syncopated rhythms that drew attention to the materiality of words—and the materiality of sense.

When Creeley began writing, a number of avant-garde artists and architects were similarly emphasizing the structural and literal qualities in their work. The steel and glass in the buildings of Mies van der Rohe, for example, revealed at every point their practical necessity. The paintings of artists like Jackson Pollock and Franz Kline were interesting for the ways in which these artists used canvas and paint, not because of their subject matter. Abstract expressionist painters, on the one hand, and architects working in the international style, on the other, were radically different from each other in virtually everything except a primary respect for the materials of their arts. In his introduction to *The Wedge,* Williams phrased the aesthetic as it applied to poetry: "A poem is a small (or large) machine made of words."[11]

Seen in context with Williams, abstract expressionism in painting, and the international style in architecture, Creeley's poetics seem very much of the 1930s and 1940s, but they have deeper roots, drawing in particular on the world of practical-minded New Englanders like Thoreau, who, for instance, demanded of architecture that it "gradually [grow] from within outward, out of the necessities and character of the indweller."[12] Thoreau struggled in his prose toward a similar end: to displace merely felicitous expression with a Yankee precision and honesty. The same may be said of Creeley.

Frost again offers an instructive comparison. Creeley and Frost are both New Englanders but New Englanders of very different kinds. Frost saw himself in the tradition of the Concord transcendentalists, but it is only the early Emerson that he resembles. Owing more to Swedenborg than either Emerson or Thoreau, he wrote in "Education by Poetry" that the "greatest of all attempts to say one thing in terms of another is the philosophical attempt to say matter in terms of spirit, or spirit in terms of matter, to make the final unity."[13] Believing this, he became a poet with transcendent truths to teach, using the sound of sense to point out moral realities that he thought existed outside, or prior

POETICS OF SOLITUDE

to, language and experience. Frost provides an obvious instance of what Olson condemned—"wisdom as such."

Creeley is much closer to Thoreau, who was striving to see and express as precisely as he could the immediate world of Walden or the Maine woods. Creeley's insistence on clarity and the particular can be found as well in the work of Emily Dickinson. She was especially concerned, as Creeley would be, with rhythm as a way of emphasizing the processes through which syntax allows meaning. She based much of her work on the metrically precise stanzas of Isaac Watts but broke her lines with dashes to interrupt the flowing cadences his manner encouraged. The sentimental certainties in which Watts specialized (and which Dickinson had known since childhood, since his hymns were commonly used in the local church) are alluring at least in part because of his mellifluous, honeyed sound, as in the following verse from "Our God, Our Help":

> Under the shadow of thy throne
> >Thy saints have dwelt secure;
> Sufficient is thine arm alone,
> >And our defense is sure.

By contrast, a great many of her poems struggle within themselves to resolve a certain problem or find its adequate expression in anguished broken lines: "Won't you wish you'd smiled — just —/ Me upon?" [14]

ROBERT CREELEY

Lines like these, much like Creeley's poems, should be read as enactments, not as imitations of ideal form. In passages like the one above, Dickinson was obviously concerned with meaning as a process, something toward which one struggled, rather than as something already known and tested.

Creeley said that when he was growing up, Dickinson "was primary and close" to him; and in a 1985 lecture on her work, he called attention to her worldliness, a quality her poetry shares with his.[15] In her work, he said, Dickinson would not deny what her senses told her was real in favor of abstractions. She saw her literal surroundings with acuity and sought exact language in which to express it— a very different ambition from Frost's "say[ing] one thing in terms of another." In Dickinson, no truths are final; no conclusions are ultimate except death. There is only what the language of the poem permits one, in a certain context, to say.[16]

According to Creeley, Emerson's "senses of how poetry takes place were crucial for American writers."[17] He was certainly crucial for Creeley, whose "attention, his curiosity and respect," as Duncan pointed out, are markedly Emersonian. Duncan says that "at first we think to find [Creeley] self-expressive," but that is not the case. He is concerned ultimately with his medium and the world, not his private affairs.[18]

In his autobiography, Creeley said that he had always considered his life something for which he had "the respon-

POETICS OF SOLITUDE

sibility"—a sense he identified as particularly characteristic of Puritans: "a curious split between the physical fact of a person and that thing they otherwise think with, or about, the so-called mind." [19] An advantage of that attitude is that it keeps one from becoming crucially absorbed in one's private dilemmas; one's life is never the whole of existence. It is somehow other, a responsibility.

Creeley is descended from an old Yankee family, although not one that played a major role in New England history. He was four years old when his father, a doctor, died. Life had been fairly comfortable for the family until that time, but money then became a concern. Nonetheless, with scholarships, Creeley was able to attend Milton Academy, a Massachusetts preparatory school patronized by old and affluent families, and to matriculate at Harvard. His college expenses were paid with money awarded for damages resulting from a freak accident that had occurred when he was two and had cost him the use of his left eye. Three years later—the child was not told what would happen until it was over—the eye was operated on and removed. This trauma and the failure of the family to explain to Creeley the finality of his father's death left him with a personal recognition of "an immense sense of my family's particular limits" (*Autobiography,* 19).

That view has a parallel in the Puritan's assumption, rooted in Calvinist theology, that life offers individual opportunities but only within a profoundly determined and limited universe. Characteristically, Creeley, sharing

ROBERT CREELEY

Olson's sense of the world as centered in each individual, took his circumstance as unique, yet there is a clear link between this view and a general pattern repeated throughout New England's history and literature. Edward Taylor's pastoral study, Thoreau's hut at Walden, Dickinson's upstairs room in Amherst, and Charles Ives's Spartan studio were not prisons but private worlds that helped to define the artist's objective. The pattern in each instance was to accept imposed (or self-imposed) limits and then to look to the imagination. Among New England artists, there are rarely the kind of complaints about the narrowness of one's circumstances that can be found among Midwestern artists, for example; nor are there assertions of grand, encompassing personality that one finds in Whitman (and, for that matter, in Olson, who proved to be an exceptional New Englander in this regard). The New England artist begins with a recognition of limits.

The New Englander understands his or her condition as personal, located in particular circumstances and revealed by experience. An individual's condition is to be accepted and also understood, and it is within these terms that one locates Creeley's retrospective response to his mother's decision not to tell him that he was going to have his eye removed: "I so wish she had told me, although I rationally understand why she did not" (*Autobiography,* 21).

Dickinson's response in such extreme situations could be equally direct and economic, refusing, for example, the

POETICS OF SOLITUDE

grand vision and satisfactions of religion. In a letter written when she was a student at Mount Holyoke Seminary (and quoted by Creeley in his 1985 lecture), she said, "I feel that the world holds a predominant place in my affections. I do not feel that I could give up all for Christ, were I called to die" ("Girl," 43). Given the religious pressures with which she was surrounded (as a Mount Holyoke student, she had to deal regularly with friends who tried to convert her and prayed for her when she failed to comply), Dickinson's statement is as determined as Creeley's. There is a refusal on the part of both to confront anything but truth, to live in anything but the world of fact. In his autobiography, Creeley wrote that he "distrusted fiction," preferring the plain distinction of "prose"—a response, he felt, that he owed to the Puritan world of his childhood, which left him with strict regard for truth (*Autobiography,* 93).

Creeley began as a writer of short stories in which he studied the capacities of language to express psychological states exactly. He published a collection of the stories, *The Gold Diggers,* on his own in 1954. A commercial edition, *The Gold Diggers and Other Stories,* was not published until 1965, by which time his reputation as a poet was well established. As a consequence, his prose is less well known than his poetry, but it is an exceedingly important part of his work.

In the 1960s, Creeley's fiction was briefly grouped with works by a few other writers as an instance of the

"New American Story," a kind of prose fiction that found a principal source in the work of Stein, and that distinction, although generally overlooked in recent accounts of American fiction, is still useful. Expressionists like Anderson were concerned mainly with ways to present character, and they took the expressive mode in Stein's *Three Lives* as their model. Writers like Creeley, however, although indebted to expressionist writing, were more interested in Stein's language experiments such as the prose poems in *Tender Buttons,* which entail a radical formalism.

In *Tender Buttons* Stein tried to find ways to give things names that were more than descriptive labels. She took ordinary subjects such as "A Piece of Coffee" and "Mildred's Umbrella" and tried to find words that would "express what [each] . . . was." The brief passages that resulted were not, she claimed, simply her impressions or free associations. To name an object, she said, a writer should find the words that were somehow "the thing in itself."[20]

In his essay on *Tender Buttons* Robert Grenier argued that Stein was concerned with language not "as object-in-itself" but as "composition functioning in the composition of the world."[21] Meaning in her work depended on an individual's coming into immediate contact with the world. Experience, not formal learning, was primary. "The business of Art," Stein concluded, ". . . is to live in the actual present, that is the complete actual present, and to completely express that complete actual present."[22] In this, the

POETICS OF SOLITUDE

prose did not describe but enact; the language was its own occasion, its own subject. As Williams said in his essay on Stein, "The words . . . transcend everything."[23]

Williams was one of Stein's persuasive disciples and also greatly important to Creeley. The successful story, Williams believed, involved "perhaps a transit from adjective (the ideal 'copy') to verb (showing process)." What he wanted was to suggest the process by which one became aware of something or did something. The result, he said, was "life, not morals. It is THE LIFE which comes alive in the telling."[24]

In his introduction to *New American Story* (1965), Warren Tallman noted that, as Williams had said, Stein had "placed writing on a plane where it may deal unhampered with its own affairs, unburdened with scientific and philosophical lumber." A writer's only guides now were "sight, sound, sense and syntax"; and each writer must deal with these matters in a personal and unique way, dependent "entirely upon his individual character, capacity and experience."[25] In "Notes for a New Prose," first published in *Origin* in 1951, Creeley argued that reality was "just that which is believed, just as long as it is, believed." Poets knew this, but he wanted to find a way in which the same principle could be expressed in fiction: "There is nothing more real, in essence, about a possible prose than there is about any possible poetry." Further, if the writer were good, he or she should be able present a conjectured situation as if it had actually happened. Experience in fiction had more to do with using language than with anything the writer had personally experienced.

Nonetheless, according to the essay, the actual shape and language of a work would be profoundly the writer's own; in the story the writer would be making "what is in himself."[26] If the incidents, in other words, were not personal, the language was deeply so. If, on the one hand, as Creeley later wrote, the speaker in a story was the language (not "I, isolated,"[27]), it was also true that storytelling gave the writer's "life a way of thinking of itself in the very fact and feeling of existence"[28]; words were more deeply of the writer than the facts of the writer's life.

Similarly, in "A Note on the Objective," Creeley pointed out that although the poet might wish to be "free of imprecise 'feeling,'" making "as complete a break as possible with the subjective," "things have to come in before they can go out." Although it was desirable to avoid the subjective insofar as it led to "emotional claptrap," writing would always be subjective in other ways (*Essays,* 463–64). This was a primary lesson to be learned from *Tender Buttons.*

Creeley's stories generally involve a single episode and depend on the perspective of one person, often a solitary individual, painfully alone, who tries to resist conditions that have trapped him or her. There is none of what he called emotional claptrap in this attempt; it is a

POETICS OF SOLITUDE

deeply personal struggle, which is not only described but is enacted in the language itself. "Mr. Blue," to cite one of the most highly regarded of Creeley's stories, opens with the kind of quirky, very personal statement that could occur in the work of any number of writers who derive from Stein: "I don't want to give you only the grotesqueness, not only what it then seemed" (*Prose,* 20). The sentence sounds as if it could have been drawn from a story by Sherwood Anderson. The narrator, like many of Anderson's narrators, repeatedly tries to explain and justify himself, but while Anderson conventionally focuses on the development of story and character, Creeley is drawn to the linguistic complexities a narrator like this can create in the process of trying to explain himself: "I suspect that you have troubles of your own, and, since you have, why bother you with more. Mine against yours. That seems a waste of time. But perhaps mine are also yours. And if that's so, you'll find me a sympathetic listener" (*Prose,* 21).

The convoluted reasoning is in a way beside the point; what matters is the difficulty it portrays in speaking in a world where one must have a "reason" for imposing oneself on another. As the story unfolds, the narrator's situation appears increasingly illogical. He struggles to make it sound sensible, and in the process his language becomes even more knotted and intense.

One might compare Creeley's narrator with Anderson's in "Death in the Woods." Anderson's narrator also repeatedly tries to justify himself, to explain why he finds it necessary to tell the story, which he remembers from his boyhood. But the story, which concerns a woman's death in the woods, contains information that the narrator could not possibly know, as there was no one there but the woman and her dogs when she died. The teller has spent many years constructing what he now insists is the true story. He wants to convince his listener and himself that he knows what in fact he could not know.

But Anderson, as is usually the case in his best work, is most concerned here with the story itself; it is in the gradual unfolding of the narrative that the work acquires force. Creeley is engaged in a similar project in "Mr. Blue," but his principal focus is the narrator's struggle to explain his actions and the convoluted, baroque diction that results. In his nervous haste to make himself clear, the narrator delivers a bizarre monologue about how dwarfs, gnomes, and midgets experience the world. Weird details and observations repeatedly intrude, as when he says his wife is big-boned and follows that by saying that this sounds as if he "were selling her" (*Prose,* 21).

Finally he gets around to the story itself, which concerns an incident that took place at a carnival he attended one night with his wife. (The fact that it is a carnival has to be deciphered from the text; the narrator is so busy explaining himself that details like this are overlooked.) They went to the freak show, although, as he has explained, he doesn't like looking at freaks or even being near them: "They seem

POETICS OF SOLITUDE

to have a particular feeling around them, which is against me, altogether" (*Prose,* 22). One of the freaks was a midget, and the barker joked with the women in the audience about whether they might like to take the midget home with them. The narrator, utterly distraught, wanted leave to the show, but the crowd pressed so close that he couldn't find his way out. At this point, the barker asked the midget which of the women he would prefer, and the midget indicated the narrator's wife, who then told her husband that she had seen the midget earlier in the day and that he had motioned toward her and done a sort of dance—which, at this moment, he suddenly did again. As soon as the show was over, the narrator cleared a path through the audience for himself and his wife, and they left.

As the narrator reaches the end of his story, his agony intensifies until his language, by this point largely monosyllabic, becomes a series of violent gestures. His distress is intensified in the prose itself, and it is the prose that is the story's real acheivement: "I looked, a flash, sideways, as it then happened. Looked, he looked at me, cut, the hate jagged, and I had gone, then, into it and that was almost that" (*Prose,* 26).

In his introduction to *The Gold Diggers,* Creeley wrote that in another age, he "would have been a moralist," but without that option, he was left simply with the fact of the tale and "whatever emotion best can serve it" (*Prose,* 11). Repeatedly, that emotion is massively convoluted, calling for intricate syntax and statement like that in "Mr. Blue."

ROBERT CREELEY

"Three Fate Tales," for example, begins, "I put it this way. That I am, say, myself, that this, or this feel, you can't have, or from that man or this, me, you can't take it" (*Prose,* 32). Creeley's narrators are often drowning men struggling for the surface. They may believe they will reach the surface, but then they plunge again and again back within themselves and drown finally in the complexities they find.

Creeley's protagonists are rarely attractive; all are so unreachably situated within their desires and needs that they have become their own masochistic victims. *The Island* (1963), a novel in which Creeley draws on the failure of his first marriage, centers on masochistic self-indulgence. Creeley writes in a note at the beginning of the book that "it is only in the relationships men manage, that they live at all" (*Prose,* 101). In some contexts this statement would be unmistakably sentimental; but the figures in *The Island* are caught in a collapsing marriage, and the "relationships men manage" in this case are anguished: "Reality [has become] the shifting face of needs" (*Prose,* 222). The marriage began with the hope that "it would be their world," but the husband and wife, John and Joan, have reached a point at which they make love only when he insists on it; and as he proceeds altogether selfishly to satisfy himself, she makes a point of not responding and falls asleep.

The implication of *The Island* is that a man indeed is, or can be, emotionally an island. When Joan almost dies from an ovarian cyst, the narrator fails to grasp the depth of

POETICS OF SOLITUDE

her anguish and pain. When she is brought back, unconscious, from the operating room, he asks (but only to himself—she is still under the influence of the anesthetic), "Who are you?," and then, although he takes her hand, he cannot "move closer" (*Prose,* 177).

The book ends with a sequence in which the narrator imagines that his wife has injured or drowned herself. He is not concerned with whatever she might have suffered but rather transforms his anguish at what he imagines to have happened into self-serving melodrama. She had left their house at night, but he thinks at first that she probably did not go far, and he tries to find her. He feels that she has done this to afflict him, that she wants him "fumbling about in the dark . . . for fear she might be hurt" (*Prose,* 238). Then in his imagination he becomes increasingly convinced that she actually might have had an accident, might perhaps have fallen from a cliff near their house and so have "left him to explain his failure, her death, to their children, to the town, to her vicious guardian who would attack him, and would take the children away from him" (*Prose,* 240).

John's anxiety is obviously immensely self-indulgent. He is able to imagine that the woman who has failed him and whom he has failed is dead, leaving him to suffer. And certainly he does suffer, but his suffering is self-induced and self-centered; to himself, he seems the greater victim. To complete the drama, he returns home, goes to his sons, and "[pulls] them, crying, into his arms." At that point he looks up and sees his wife holding their daughter. She asks him what is wrong. His response is appropriately flat, without any indication that he might be relieved to find her alive: "I thought you were dead... but I was wrong" (*Prose,* 241).

Creeley has repeatedly insisted that in his works he is primarily interested in language itself. In his interview with Michael André he said that he felt "writing is primarily the experience of language, and diversity of contexts, and diversity of changes and significations. I'm frankly and selfishly interested in words."[29] One of the clearest instances of this is provided by the collection of prose pieces known as *Mabel: A Story.* The book is divided into three parts, the first of which, "A Day Book," is a set of journal entries from 19–30 November 1968 and 14 January–27 February 1969.[30] While there is not an entry for each day, there are enough to give a fairly clear and intimate view of the narrator's day-to-day life.

The second section, "Presences: A Text for Marisol," was written to accompany a book of Marisol's photographs but was dropped by the publisher, who apparently had expected critical commentaries and got instead a series of prose passages one to three pages long. Most are anecdotal reminiscences. The third section, "Mabel: A Story," is similarly arranged; its subjects are various women Creeley had known.

The model for *Mabel: A Story,* aside from conventional journals and classics like Sei Shonagon's pillow book, may

POETICS OF SOLITUDE

be prose pieces by Jack Kerouac such as "October in the Railroad Earth." Kerouac called his technique in works like these "sketching"—recording an immediate verbal response to a subject. One would choose a subject and then let the words follow in whatever order they might. The writing would consequently display candor, openness, and immediacy; since such writing was spontaneous, it would be more likely to express the writer's genuine response to a situation than would a more considered work. By following this method, Creeley was able to create in *Mabel* a kind of autobiography; the book is filled with personal information and anecdotes, but even more significant is the range of emotions the pieces gave him an opportunity to display. The real subject of the book is the enormous complexity of Creeley as a person and as a writer.

If *Mabel: A Story* has a moral center, it is in the repeated recognition that one should not trust one's private assumptions and that the world is always a better guide than one's self to the nature of things. Creeley observes, for example, that "coincident with consciousness is an ability not only to know things, but to recognize and anticipate *feelings,* even to propose them, the terror or pleasure in that act notwithstanding, so that the reality so engendered becomes the experience of the world entirely" (*Prose,* 360).

Creeley is saying that one's "experience of the world" can be completely self-proposed—which is exactly the notion that stories like "Mr. Blue" explore. He follows the statement with an account of a visit by a husband and wife to the Villa Serbelloni, the Rockefeller Research Institute at Bellagio on Lake Como. Creeley gives all the guidebook details about the history and the landscape; the couple are living in the kind of sublime landscape that drew English and American Romantics to Italy, but their immediate obsession is a sordid argument they are having with each other. At the end of the piece, however, the husband says that as he sat writing, he heard an outboard motor and voices and laughter coming from a distance; none of those who had made the place so famous was now, he says, "more actual." The sketch ends with his realization that it is "best that one's needs be simple" (*Prose,* 364). That is at least an antidote to fictions about one's self and one's world. Creeley's point is that we should trust the factual and concrete rather than the imagination; as Williams had said, "No ideas but in things."

The narrator of Creeley's poem "The Whip," in bed beside his sleeping wife, thinks of a woman he would rather be with. Feeling sorry for himself, he cries out, and when his wife reaches to comfort him, he says, "I think to say this / wrongly"—to say something that might please her but that would not be true (*CP,* 146).

Similarities between poems like "The Whip" and stories like "Mr. Blue" are obvious but superficial. Creeley's poems, even more than his fiction, turn on formal and technical questions. Although "Mr. Blue" is finally interesting because of the complexities in its language, it also

POETICS OF SOLITUDE

involves an acute psychological dissection. In *The Island* and *Mabel: A Story,* the psychological curiosity is even more prominent; it dominates the novel. Creeley's essay on "The Whip," on the other hand, makes it clear that, whatever the poem's psychological interest, he was concerned mainly with questions of formal construction—matters such as cadence and sound.

Creeley's poems are intricate and precise assemblages, but it is far from adequate, in Williams's analogy, to see them simply as well-constructed machines. A better comparison was suggested by Gustaf Sobin, who compared a Creeley poem with a waterfall—"the lines themselves like so many ledges and the poem, the thrust of the poem, like a waterfall, falling down over those ledges, splashing, plummeting as it does." [31]

Psychology and form are inseparable both in Creeley's poetry and in his prose ("The logic of . . . his content," Creeley wrote to Olson, can be the poet/speaker's "method, his form" [32]), but in his poems, the movement of words is a much greater urgency. "I think somehow poetry includes certainly the attitudes and feelings one has," said Creeley elsewhere, "but they are not the particular point." [33] What matters is the movement, the shaping thrust of rhythm and syntax.

Creeley's concentration on formal matters distinguishes his work from that of such immediate predecessors as Kenneth Fearing, Kenneth Patchen, Muriel Rukeyser, and Kenneth Rexroth, who were concerned with poetry as

ROBERT CREELEY

communication, as a vehicle for politics, metaphysical speculation, and spiritual matters. Although Creeley was always distant in his poetics from traditionalists among such contemporaries as Wilbur, the early Lowell, and Berryman, he was like them a formalist of the sort that New Critics celebrated in the 1940s and 1950s, when he began writing. Compared to what one finds in "The Kingfishers" or Duncan's sequence "The Structure of Rime," much of Creeley's poetry contains very conventional structuring devices and techniques. Although Creeley adopted Olson's projective poetics in the 1960s and 1970s, his other poetry, in spite of its rhythms and unusual line breaks, is traditionally shaped, often in couplets or quatrains, and it is occasionally rhymed. It is an orderly poetry that moves to closure and often deals with conventional themes.

Creeley is also a lyrical poet—indeed, in the poems collected in *The Charm* and *For Love,* he is probably the best love poet of his generation. He is so adamant in claiming that what matters in the poem is not its subject but its language, one hesitates to label him in this way, but among his contemporaries none has so often adopted, and at the same time so fully transformed, the love poem—the most conventional of all kinds of lyric poetry. As recast by Creeley, however, the love poem is very far from its traditional expression; his anxieties are not as simple as those of the troubadour or the cavalier, for whom the beloved was, at worst, indifferent to the poet's attention.

POETICS OF SOLITUDE

Love in Creeley's poetry is marked by peculiarly modern situations and anxiety and tension. The speaker in these poems, like the speaker in "Mr. Blue," is often defeated by his subjectivity and his desire for an ideal that contemporary life will never provide. These poems can be quite caustic. In "Love," for example, the speaker says that love is like a squirrel and a cat that he has seen—one bleeding, the other "somehow immaculate" (*CP,* 19). The speaker in "The Mirror" says that the belief that there can be love is belief in "the incredible" (*CP,* 37). Another poem, also titled "Love," begins:

> Not enough. the question: what is.
> Given: grace[.]
>
> (*CP,* 26)

In his poems Creeley returns again and again to the disjunction between who people really are and the fraudulent impressions they give each other. Sentiment is seen as a "trap" (*CP,* 57), and so is laughter, which, according to "The Crisis," may get rid of "rancor" but does not make one act any more mercifully toward another. The conclusion of "For Irving" is that men and women simply reach an "agreement" (*CP,* 64).

"The Bed" begins with Byron's line "She walks in beauty" but then becomes a satire on domesticity, its hypocrisies and unrealistic expectations. Whitman's line

ROBERT CREELEY

"Out of the Cradle endlessly rocking" becomes "Out of the table endlessly rocking"; the poem is about marital discord and ends with the bitter assertion "Everything is water / if you look long enough" (*CP,* 163). In "Wait for Me," a husband lectures his wife that the "*essential / hypocrisies*" are necessary (*CP,* 137).

Not all of the love poems are bitter or despondent, but very few treat love purely as joy. Among the exceptions, "Kore" concerns the recovery of innocence that love can bring with it; freed at last from Hades, Kore lets herself be led without anger, resistance, or distrust toward whatever love has next for her (*CP,* 206). "The Sentence" is an elaborate conceit in which love is viewed as a kind of "syntax" and a desire for "a continuity, a place." But these poems are exceptions: Creeley is much more likely to be concerned with the traps of false and superficial emotion, role-playing, or the failure to be an adequate husband or wife.

The troubled emotions in these poems about love are, as in the stories, voiced in conflicting rhythms and syntax. Creeley's poems are structured like the films of Sergei Eisenstein; both depend on inner friction and struggle—between images in Eisenstein, between words in Creeley. Olson's poems, by contrast, work in a manner more common in conventional films, which give the impression of fluid continuity (or, to quote "Projective Verse," "One perception . . . immediately and directly lead[s] to a further

POETICS OF SOLITUDE

perception" [34]). There are very powerful moments of rhythmic conflict in Olson's work, but a progressive cadence is more common.

In addition to elaborate rhythmic complexities, Creeley's poems, particularly the early ones, frequently employ convoluted grammar and syntax. Here, for example, is a passage from "The Sentence":

> There is that in love
> which, by the syntax of,
> men find women and join
> their bodies to their minds[.]
>
> (*CP,* 95)

The complete syntax frustrates any simple interpretation. Does the poem say that men join the bodies of women "to their minds," and if so, whose minds—their own or the men's? Does the poem claim that men think for women? (Since "The Sentence" dates from the 1950s, that sexist reading seems a likely possiblity.) Or do the men, in finding the women, thereby find the means to make themselves whole? Grammar, rhythm, syntax are all tense and unsettled, and the result is an exceedingly intricate instance of poetic energy.

It would be difficult and exhausting to maintain such conflicts in a long poem; Creeley's poems, so fraught with inner struggles, continually threaten to break apart; they require a counterthrust (a regular series of stanzas, for example, or equally measured lines) to contain the competing energies. One result is that almost all of his early poems are brief and sharply contained—at least until *Pieces* (1968), in which, significantly, the rhythms are less violent.

In his poems as in his prose works, Creeley is puritanical in his scrupulous attention to personal inadequacies, examining desires and motives much as John Winthrop does in his journal or Edward Taylor does in his poetry. Despite his claims not to be a moralist, Creeley is exactly that in both poems and prose. The poems are obsessed with personal inadequacy and guilt, and many are concerned at some point, like Puritan autobiography, with the anguish occasioned by the insufficiencies and inadequacies that the speaker finds in himself.

This intense self-examination and honesty contribute much to Creeley's reconception of the love poem. Conventionally the poet declares that the love poem is a tribute to the beloved, conferring in the process a kind of immortality, although in fact the beloved is rarely characterized in the work itself. The only one immortalized in any meaningful way is the writer. What does Petrarch actually say of Laura?

In "The Door," one of Creeley's most intricate and highly regarded love poems, he writes about following through life a woman whom he addresses as "Lady." He

POETICS OF SOLITUDE

will never catch up to her, he says; she will be known to him only by the flash of a skirt as she disappears through a doorway. But she does not have to be a genuine person. As he reveals, with perfect candor, what matters is the pursuit and the joys and sufferings it entails; it is these that give him the grounds to "go on talking forever" (*CP*, 201). The "Lady" is his door to the poem. The core of Creeley's poetics is here: experience becomes essentially a source for the work rather than its own importance.

Words and *Pieces,* Creeley's two major collections of works from the 1960s, focus on the operations of language and ways it which it generates its own meaning. In a prefatory note to *Words,* Creeley said that his "various purposes will not understand . . . [words] more than what they say" (*CP*, 261). The corollary is that words may very well resist saying what the poet wants them to say. "Waiting" concerns a man who tries to push the words in certain directions, much as if they were boulders, but they resist, and he is left "disturbed and fumbling" (*CP*, 270).

Words includes a series of poems dealing with the pronoun *I*. The first of these, simply titled "I," gives factual genealogical and geographical information about Creeley's background; this is the *I* that is defined by the literal conditions in which one is found, but that *I* is at best a kind of historical fact, something in a census or a family history. At the end of the poem, Creeley says that his father bought himself a grave so that he could not be dug up—so that, in other words, he could not be given identification or purpose by the world again: at last they would have to leave that *I* alone.

The *I* in "Internals," on the other hand, finds its identity according to its place in the natural world—the sunlight, the lake, the trees by which the *I* is surrounded—but the issue is the same: the *I* is dependent on the world in which it finds itself.

A third dependence is in language itself, a dependence which Creeley explores in "The Pattern":

> As soon as
> I speak, I
> speaks.
>
> (*CP,* 294)

What is this *I,* and why does it speak—"to / hear myself / speak?" Creeley asks (*CP,* 294). And is there a deeper reason? The *I* is a redundancy, naming itself. In similar fashion, "Intervals" asserts that the *I* is simply "identity / singing" (*CP,* 365). "Words / say everything," but there has to be a speaker: "Speech is a mouth" (*CP,* 283). Speech is then presence, the way in which the *I* asserts itself in the world.

"In a book like *Words,*" Creeley said, "I began trying to think of ways in which I could break habits of writing and

POETICS OF SOLITUDE

composition," but the "key book" was *Pieces,* in which "the concept of poems as set instances of articulate statement yields to a sense of continuity."[35] Many of the early works involve a struggle toward some resolution or closure—a sudden recognition or insight that can bring the poem to an end.

Pieces is not the series of miscellaneous notations that it may at first seem; together the notations indicate a range of feeling. The book coheres in much the same way as *Mabel: A Story:* things are held together not by narrative structure but by one sensibility expressing its multifold nature. It is not that one poem proposes the next, although sometimes that happens, but that they all cohere as parts of one field of awareness. This is "composition by field," as Olson had defined it in "Projective Verse"—the presentation of a particular order but a set of illuminations that, taken together, suggest a spatial rather than causal relation to each other.[36]

In *Pieces* and the book that followed, *A Day Book,* Creeley pursued what Ginsberg, in describing his own poetry, called a "sequence of thought-forms passing naturally through ordinary mind."[37] Some critics who had admired Creeley's earlier formal work were not pleased. M. L. Rosenthal, for example, criticized *A Day Book* for what seemed to him "a loose and stumbling casualness."[38] Whatever Creeley was doing, he was obviously not "stumbling"; it was simply a different kind of project he was working on, one that required a serious playfulness and a spontaneous energy. Such qualities are demonstrated in the following passage from "Numbers":

> *We are seven*, echoes in
> my head like a nightmare of
> responsibility—seven
> days in the week, seven
> years for the itch of
> unequivocal involvement.
>
> (*CP,* 401)

The passage begins as an elaborate but dark joke: the child in Wordsworth's poem "We Are Seven" has a true "nightmare of responsibility" since members of his family have died and so exist only in his imagination; if he forgets them, then they will be gone forever. We are, the poem suggests, responsible for remembering the dead; they live literally because we keep them in mind. The associations that follow in Creeley's poem are generally grim. Remembering the fact that he was born at 7:00 A.M. triggers thoughts of the death of his father, who is remembered now, not by a child like the one in Wordsworth's poem, but by a stone monument "at the entrance of the / hospital, of which he was head" (*CP,* 401).

The poems in these books are as precisely articulated as any in Creeley's work but avoid much of textual complexi-

POETICS OF SOLITUDE

ties of the earlier poems. Some of the most successful are minimalist exercises worked out in monosyllables. For example,

> You want
> the fact
> of things
> in words,
> of words.

(CP, 429)

In the 1970s, Creeley's poetry changed again, returning to traditional, formal structures, but this time taking its model from the elegy rather than the love poem. There are many love poems in the later works, but the dominant tone is elegiac, particularly in the strongest books, such as *Windows* and *Memory Gardens,* which are really extended meditations on solitude and loss. To cite one particularly effective poem, "Scales" in *Windows* evokes an inner world of "such small dimension" with "world shrunk // to some recollected / edge of where it used to be."

Many of these poems deal with the death of friends and members of Creeley's family. In "Four Years Later," for example, he regrets not having been closer to his mother. Her world is gone; even her possessions have been dispersed. He remembers her voice and certain words she used but then recalls the value she placed on discretion, her need to hide her feelings behind the ordinary. Her inner life, as a result, was always shut to others, including the poet, and he knows she would never have allowed the familiarity he wishes they had shared.

In "Things To Do In Providence," Ted Berrigan had written,

The heart stops briefly when someone dies,
a quick pain as you hear the news, & someone passes
from your outside life to inside. Slowly the heart adjusts
to its new weight, & slowly everything continues, sanely.[39]

Creeley adopted this "sane" response to irrational loss in his own work, notably in his elegy for Berrigan. "Things to do today," he wrote, are "left empty":

> It's all moved inside,
> all that dear world[.][40]
>
> (*CP*, 39)

The "presence" of those who have died, says Creeley in "Bookcase," has "become a resonance" (*Memory Gardens,* 30). In "Oh Max," he concludes, "Better remember / / all one can forever—/ never, *never* forget."[41]

The last section of *Windows* is a sequence entitled "Helsinki Window," which Creeley wrote while he was living in Finland during the late 1980s. It is one of his most

POETICS OF SOLITUDE

successful later works, a culmination of more than a decade of poems on isolation and loss. The first poem suggests an inner world in which the speaker can feel safe and unthreatened, but at the same time he is largely isolated, without any deep contact with those around him. In the second of the poems, he says with amusement that he "recognizes, at last, by god, / he's not all there is"; but at the same time, as he reminds himself, *"Now you're inside entirely."* [42]

The subjects of these poems include the city of Helsinki, its geography, and its weather. The poems are tranquil and accepting, quite unlike the earlier poems, but nothing ever fully dissolves the feeling of ultimate solitude they convey. The sequence ends with cautious optimism, however, in "Spring Light," in which the poet speaks of "wonders come again," bringing "pieces of what had not been lost" (*Windows,* 150).

In the spring of 1990, a session titled "Robert Creeley and the Politics of Person" was held as part of a symposium at the St. Mark's Church Poetry Project in New York. The session was organized by Barrett Watten, who argued in his introductory remarks that "Creeley's work is resolutely organized around a biographical axis—the occasion of writing is continually proposed as an experience in or of a lifetime brought to transcendent and inherent particularity in the poem. But while autobiography—while formally aligned—may be the work's framing, and ultimately one of its primary values, the particulars of the poem itself often work to undermine the stability of person, to set it in doubt."[43]

One of the speakers was Susan Howe, herself a poet firmly within the New England tradition and one of the principal contemporary poets whose work is rooted in Black Mountain aesthetics. Howe began by acknowledging the critical fashion that claims, in the wake of Sausurrean linguistics and structuralism, the death of the author and subjectivity. She turned then to "Experience," in which Emerson argued, in her words, that sense-experience and life are rivals. Bodies never really come in contact. We are alienated even from our own sorrow. Our waking intellects are baffled before some cause that refuses to be named. Impressions are apparitions. We see mediately. Nature has no memory. Anything holds true. We are fragments."[44]

In describing Emerson's position, Howe was describing Creeley's. The modern thing to do, Howe suggested, would be to join the structuralists in their nihilism, but instead, Creeley, like Emily Dickinson, continued searching: "In their poems America is still unexplored and unsettled." Rather than being resolved, defeated, to the barrenness behind the structuralist's scenario, she said, Creeley pursues his "American philosophical investigations." Of course, a unique cadence and music imply solitude. "American poets," she concluded, "are solitaries who go in company."[45]

POETICS OF SOLITUDE

Although it may be true that the self and subjectivity are fictions—constructions, that is, in and of language—cadence, music, and the patterns of meaning that they embody can be both sensual and individual, varying immensely from poet to poet. Each poet's unique identity may at the least be evident in the sensual texture and process of his or her words. Not every poet would agree with Williams's claim that "the only world that exists is the world of the senses" [46]—but that premise is a given in Black Mountain poetry.

Isolation may be unavoidable for some, but it can become either a source of anguish or a source of poems. "I live in an angle of a leaden wall," wrote Thoreau, who valued his solitude but looked with some arrogance toward whatever was beyond his shell, "into whose composition was poured a little alloy of bell metal. Often, in the repose of my mid-day, there reaches my ears a confused *tintinnabulation* from without. It is the noise of my contemporaries." [47]

There is none of Thoreau's arrogance in Creeley, but he shares with his predecessor a firm—and moral—recognition of the difference between public and private speech. In solitude there is indeed salvation. "Language has, publicly," he wrote, "become such an instrument of coercion, persuasion, and deceit. The power thus collected is ugly beyond description—it is truly *evil*. And it will not go away.

ROBERT CREELEY

"Trust to good verses then . . . Trust to the clarity instant in being human, that knows and wants no other place" (*Essays,* 578).

Notes

1. Robert Hass, "Creeley: His Metric," *Twentieth Century Pleasures: Prose on Poetry* (New York: Ecco, 1984) 150; David L. Elliott, An Interview with Robert Creeley," *Sagetrieb* 10 (Spring/Fall 1991): 57.

2. William Carlos Williams, *The Collected Earlier Poems* (New York: New Directions, 1966) 344.

3. Hass, 151.

4. Juan Amador Bedford, "A Poetics of Use: William Carlos Williams and Robert Creeley," *Revista Canaria de Estudios Ingleses* 13/14 (April 1987): 220–21.

5. Creeley, *The Collected Poems: 1945–1975* (Berkeley: University of California Press, 19822) 3320. Further references will be noted parenthetically in the text as *CP*.

6. Hass, 151.

7. Charles Bernstein, *Content's Dream: Essays 1975–1984* (Los Angeles: Sun & Moon Press, 1986) 294.

8. Elliott, 58.

9. Hass, 150.

10. Lawrence Thompson, *Robert Frost: The Early Years, 1874–1915* (New York: Holt, Rinehart and Winston, 1966) 418.

11. Williams, *Selected Essays* (New York: New Directions, 1954) 256. 12. Henry David Thoreau, *Walden* (Princeton: Princeton University Press, 1971) 47.

POETICS OF SOLITUDE

13. Robert Frost, "Education by Poetry," *Selected Prose of Robert Frost,* ed. Hyde Cox and Edward C. Lathem (New York: Collier, 1968) 35.

14. Emily Dickinson, *The Complete Poems,* ed. Thomas H. Johnson (Boston: Little, Brown, 1960) 347.

15. Robert Creeley, "The Girl Next Door," *Ironwood* 28 (Fall 1986): 38, 43. Further references will be noted parenthetically in the text as "The Girl."

16. There have been repeated attempts, of course, to read Dickinson as if her poetry were essentially a substitute for political or metaphysical discourse. The best reply to these is Susan Howe's *My Emily Dickinson* (Berkeley: North Atlantic, 1985). Howe is concerned with Dickinson within poetic traditions her work itself defines.

17. Quoted in William Packard, *The Poet's Craft* (New York: Paragon, 1987) 165–66.

18. Robert Duncan, *Fictive Certainties* (New York: New Directions, 1985) 228.

19. Creeley, *Autobiography* (New York and Madras: Hanuman Books, 1990) 7, 14. Further references will be noted parenthetically in the text.

20. Gertrude Stein, *Lectures in America* (Boston: Beacon, 1985) 190.

21. Robert Grenier, "Tender Buttons," *The L=A=N=G=U=A=G=E Book,* ed. Bruce Andrews and Charles Bernstein (Carbondale and Edwardsville: Southern Illinois University Press, 1984) 206.

22. Stein, 104–5.

23. Williams, *Selected Essays,* 117.

24. Williams, *Selected Essays,* 303, 309.

25. Warren Tallman, *New American Story* (New York: Grove Press, 1965) 4.

26. Creeley, *The Collected Essays* (Berkeley and Los Angeles: University of California Press, 1989) 466. Further references will be noted parenthetically in the text as *Essays.*

27. Quoted in Tallman, 264.

28. Creeley, *Collected Prose* (Berkeley and Los Angeles: University of California Press, 1988) 8. Further references will be noted parenthetically in the text as *Prose.*

29. Michael André, "An Interview with Robert Creeley," in Creeley, *Contexts of Poetry: Interviews 1961–1971,* ed. Donald Allen (Bolinas, Calif.: Four Seasons Foundation, 1973) 194.

30. The entries are dated here but were not in the earlier version published in *Pieces.*

31. Edward Foster, "An Interview with Gustaf Sobin," *Talisman: A Journal of Contemporary Poetry and Poetics* 10 (Spring 1993): 31.

32. Robert Olson and Creeley, *The Complete Correspondence,* vol. 1, ed. George F. Butterick (Santa Barbara, Calif.: Black Sparrow Press, 1980) 118.

33. Creeley and Robert Sheppard, "Stories: Being an Information: An Interview," *Robert Creeley: The Poet's Workshop,* ed. Carroll F. Terrell (Orono, Maine: National Poetry Foundation, 1984) 56.

34. Olson, *Human Universe and Other Essays* (New York: Grove, 1967) 17.

35. Quoted in Ekbert Faas, "Interview: Robert Creeley," *Towards a New American Poetics: Essays and Interviews* (Santa Barbara, Calif.: Black Sparrow Press, 1979) 186.

36. Olson, *Human Universe,* 52.

37. Allen Ginsberg, *Collected Poems: 1947–1980* (New York: Harper & Row, 1984), xx.

38. M. L. Rosenthal, "Problems of Robert Creeley," in *Robert Creeley's Life and Work: A Sense of Increment,* ed. John Wilson (Ann Arbor: University of Michigan Press, 1987) 269.

39. Ted Berrigan, *So Going Around Cities* (Berkeley: Blue Wind Press, 1980), 260.

40. Creeley, *Memory Gardens* (New York: New Directions, 1986) 39. Further references will be noted parenthetically in the text.

41. Creeley, *Mirrors* (New York: New Directions, 1983) 84.

42. Creeley, *Windows* (New York: New Directions, 1990) 120. Further references will be noted parenthetically in the text.

43. Barrett Watten, "Robert Creeley and 'the Person,' " *Poetics Journal* 9 (1991): 140.

44. Susan Howe, "Robert Creeley and the Politics of Person," *Poetics Journal* 9 (1991): 153.

45. Howe, 155, 158.

46. Williams, *Selected Essays,* 196.

47. Thoreau, 329.

CHAPTER FOUR

Robert Duncan:
Aspirations of the Word

I compose what I call myself from a world. So for me there is a question: Is there a me? I? What I do is that I pose a creative process in which I assemble me from the surrounding facts including the body and so forth.
—**Robert Duncan, quoted in** *Towards a New American Poetics*, **ed. Ekbert Faas**

There is no place outside the work for the eternal ones of the work to stand.
—**Duncan,** *A Great Admiration: H. D./Robert Duncan Correspondence 1950–1961.*

Olson accused Duncan of pursuing "wisdom as such," but this wisdom was only "pretentious fictions," Duncan said. Duncan felt that Olson was "so keen upon the *virtu* of reality that he rejects my 'wisdom' not as it might seem at first glance because 'wisdom' is a vice; but because my wisdom is not real wisdom."[1]

Behind Duncan's remark is his recognition that Olson was himself a dispenser of wisdom, and in fact Olson's Maximus is preeminently a sage and teacher, drawn to political and economic matters: it is the wisdom of the marketplace. Olson cited "wise" intellects in his work—scholars, philosophers, prophets—but they were important largely insofar as they contributed to his social vision. Those to whom Duncan was drawn, on the other hand, were more likely to interest him because their thought, whether or not practical or "true," was striking in itself, thus providing material for poems. "Thought," Duncan wrote, "is a melody" (*FC*, 180).

One of Duncan's fullest responses to the sort of questions Olson raised is in a special Duncan issue of *Audit* published in 1967. The immediate subject of the issue was a disagreement between Duncan and Robin Blaser over their respective translations of Gérard de Nerval's *Chimeras*, but the occasion gave Duncan the opportunity to clarify his poetics: "the poem," he wrote, "is thought of as participating in a reality larger than my own, the reality of man's experience in terms of language and literature." Meanings in the work were consequently not personal; "I work in meanings which I receive or find in research." Earlier in the article he had said, "I am not, as I have perhaps tediously reiterated, 'my own poet,' but, like Nerval, I seek to find my Self in the terms of a confluence of traditions that my faith follows toward the real in the commune of man's numbers, images, names."[2] Wisdom was then one of the properties with which he worked, like numbers, images, and names; it was a property of the poem, and to the poet, that was its only value.

ROBERT DUNCAN

Born in Oakland, California, in February 1919, Robert Duncan was originally named Edward Howard Duncan. His mother died in childbirth, and his father put him in an orphanage. He was adopted the following summer by Edwin and Minnehaha Symmes, who had chosen him because they found his astrological chart favorable. They renamed him Robert Edward Symmes, which remained his legal name for the rest of his life. He adopted the name Robert Duncan only when his work began appearing in nationally distributed magazines.

Duncan grew up in a household in which matters like astrology and seances were taken very seriously. The Symmeses were Theosophists, followers of Madame Blavatsky, and they shaped their lives according to messages from the spirit world. They read authors like Shakespeare and Emerson as if their works encoded Hermetic truths—which in some ways they did. Frances Yates has traced the Hermetic tradition in Shakespeare, and Emerson had absorbed it in part (most significantly the doctrine of correspondence) through Swedenborg. When Emerson wrote that the poet would find the poem by "resigning himself to the divine *aura* which breathes through forms, and accompanying that," he was, in the eyes of Duncan's parents, casting the poet in the role of a medium.

Emerson's poetics became fundamental for Duncan; "I am, in any event, Emersonian," he declared, adding that his Emerson was not the sunny optimist but the Gnostic fatal-

ASPIRATIONS OF THE WORD

ist, submitting to "whatever happens in the course of writing as revelation—not from an unconscious, but from a spiritual world" (*FC,* 227). That spiritual world, for Duncan, was the world of poetry. One invoked Shelley or Dante to find provocations for new poems much as the medium called on voices "beyond the veil of Isis." Similarly, Raleigh and Southwell spoke again in Duncan's "A Seventeenth Century Suite in Homage to the Metaphysical Genius in English Poetry."[3] Poetry had its source in the "scales of the marvelous," where the work of one poet could merge or, as Duncan said, "rime" with the work of another. Duncan's "Thank You for Love" rimes, in this sense, with Creeley's abrupt short lines; "A New Poem (for Jack Spicer)" speaks in Spicer's dry, ironic manner and therefore "rimes" with it. To be a "derivative" poet, as Duncan repeatedly called himself, one had to recognize correspondences or rimes between one's own voice and the voice of other poets, and that was a source of poetic ecstacy: "O cave of resemblances," Duncan wrote in "The Structure of Rime XIV," "cave of rimes!"[4] Just as the Theosophist assumed that the universe was held together in a vast web of correspondences, so Duncan believed that all poetry, indeed all art, participated in a single grand system.

Theosophy implies an essentially Gnostic poetics, a Neoplatonic posture that proposes a stable, ideal universe. The real, such as the body, decays, but not the realm of "unrealities, fantasies, mere ideas." ("All ages are contemporaneous," Pound had asserted, and Duncan agreed, for they were all spun out of the same grand system of "fantasies."[5])

Duncan's task as a poet began with the links in that system and its web of correspondences; it was his work to make them manifest. So in "Nel Mezzo Del Cammin Di Nostra Vita," he says that Simon Rodilla, creator of the three Watts towers, is inseparable from his work, "a trinity upraised by himself" (*RB,* 22), but the title of the poem, which is also the opening line of Dante's *Divine Comedy,* rimes Rodilla's achievement with Dante's. In the poem, Duncan quotes Olson's warning in "Against Wisdom As Such" not to distinguish wisdom from experience. Abstracted, wisdom leads to theology and religion. Dante's theology is certified by his experience rather than by books, and Rodilla's towers are morally as well as literally "taller than the Church." But the towers, and the *Divine Comedy,* are also greater than their creators. As art, they draw their perfection not merely from experience but also from "the scales of the marvelous."

Duncan's poetry is like the astrologer's celestial map, the Zodiac, in which stars separated by vast distances seem linked in a visual and metaphysical order: certain stars form the shape of Sagittarius, the archer, while others form Capricorn—configurations that are believed to be intimately related to one's fate. The universe is coherent, but in ways only an adept can understand. Duncan knew well the power that beliefs like that could have; his own fate as a child had depended on it. To the rationalist, the Zodiac

ASPIRATIONS OF THE WORD

was nonsense, but for those to whom it was as real as the seasons, it discredited a Melvillean view of an indifferent universe and gave one a place in universal harmony.

The Zodiac's reality depended on words; it had a fictive power. It was not in itself true, but the experience of universal harmony to which it led was undeniably felt by believers. If astrology, Hermeticism, Gnosticism, and other arcane beliefs had no ground in the real world, their effects were real enough; transcendence and transfiguration were as actual as sunlight. Duncan's poetry depends as much as astrology on this fictive power. In a similar fashion, his companion Jess Collins used it in collage, and their friend Kenneth Anger, who had studied Aleister Crowley's theories of magic, used it in films. Blavatsky and Crowley may have been charlatans, but their ideas could be traced to antiquity, and they were ideas that had repeatedly emerged to strengthen and transform art. Theosophy was a relay through which a complex of feelings and beliefs reached the present.

Duncan's poetry belongs in the tradition of Gnostic revelation, Neoplatonism, and *trobar clus*—the tradition of Dante, Pico della Mirandola, Marsilio Ficino, Shakespeare's *Tempest,* orphism, Mallarmé, symbolism, Rilke, Yeats, and much more. In American culture, the Hermetic tradition is to be found as much in Stein, seeking the true names of things in *Tender Buttons,* as it is in Thoreau, interpreting his life as an inlet to moral seas; but in Duncan's work the tradition reveals its roots, acknowledges the doctrine of correspondence openly, and consequently leaves many readers, like Olson, ill at ease. Yet as Duncan realized, Hermeticism was a very broad stream, broad enough to include even Olson's primary authorities such as Jung, whose later career was deeply affected by Hermetic studies, and Whitehead, whom Duncan read essentially as a Gnostic. In "The H. D. Book" he pointed to Whitehead's statement in *Aims of Education* that "the communion of saints is a great and inspiring assemblage, but it has only one possible hall of meeting, and that is, the present." This clearly echoes the doctrine of correspondence.[6]

During the 1940s and 1950s, Duncan was a principal figure in the Bay Area poetry community, where his association with the Hermetic Brotherhood was less problematic than it later was for Olson, to whom San Francisco was "an école des Sages ou Mages as ominous as Ojai, L.A."[7] There was William Everson, who had been brought up as a Christian Scientist but had then become a pantheist under the influence of Robinson Jeffers and had finally converted to Catholicism, joined the Dominican order, and developed a poetics of erotic mysticism. Kenneth Rexroth had taken Jacob Boehme as his spiritual guide (and Boehme was another thinker who had absorbed Hermetic lessons) and been influenced by Eastern, particularly Buddhist, religious thought. Jack Spicer's poetics, traceable to Mallarmé and ultimately to alchemical and Gnostic traditions, advocated a poetry of dictation in which the poet was,

ASPIRATIONS OF THE WORD

to use Spicer's analogy, only a "radio," receiving poems from a source outside himself. Among Bay Area poets, Duncan's theosophical background was simply another means through which the poet could get beyond the restraints of rationalist thought and common sense.

Olson, more interested in particle physics than Gnostic texts, had no use for Duncan's "wisdom," but his own poetics and Duncan's intersected in the belief that the poem should avoid "the lyrical interference of the individual as ego."[8] Theosophy assumed that Truth could be found by those who understood the secret code and could see beyond the veil of Isis, but the truth that was found was never merely personal. From a radically different direction, that is, Duncan had arrived at the same point that Olson and Creeley did—namely that the poem could be much more than lyrical expression.

Theosophy implied fatalism. If one believed, like Duncan's parents, that the world of the spirit influenced the everyday world, then one was no longer fully in control of one's life. Mediums and horoscopes could tell what the universe had in store, but they could not change the future. To be wise was to know one's destiny. One of Blavatsky's cardinal beliefs was that the individual and the individual will could not be trusted; authority was cosmic and abstract ("H. D. Book" I.5, 8).

Emerson was equally a fatalist, believing the universe was gathered in a single coherence over which an individual had no control. "Let us build altars to the Beautiful Necessity," he wrote in "Fate," "which secures that all is made of one piece."[9] It was Emerson the fatalist who attracted Duncan. At the core in the work of both Duncan and Emerson is a willingness to submit to some grandly conceived power. For Emerson, that power is the Oversoul. For Duncan, it is tradition.

This is evident even in Duncan's early works. These consist, he said, of "forms embodying or expressing the content of an inner psychological drama" (*FC,* 30), but the forms themselves were derived from other poets, and whatever private emotion the work expressed, it was qualified by mannerisms and styles drawn from his reading. Eventually it was tradition that intrigued him rather than the opportunity to use the poem for personal statement. And once he had turned his attention there, he was concerned with the power of language as such. "As I write, the writing talks to me" (*FC,* 125), he said.

Browning was one of the first poets to interest Duncan. Browning's dramatic monologues showed him how to manipulate language to invoke a presence or voice other than his own. Browning had practiced a kind of spiritualist's art; he was a medium through whom a range of characters spoke, and yet the poems all had his own characteristic diction and cadences.[10] In the "Stein Imitations," Duncan would push Browning's poetics further until the poet's voice was virtually obscured in the voice of the person speaking through him.

ASPIRATIONS OF THE WORD

Duncan's interest in Browning was part of a general concern with poetics of dictation—poetics that required submission to voices beyond the poet's will or intention. As a young poet, Duncan was interested in automatic writing, for example, and he attentively read poets whose work was dictated, such as William Butler Yeats and Rainer Maria Rilke.

Duncan was also, paradoxically, an anarchist "in the tradition of Emerson and Thoreau."[11] The politics may have been at least in part a response to his homosexuality, for anarchists were in Duncan's youth among the very few who did not condemn homosexuals as pariahs. At Berkeley, he had a group of friends—the artist Virginia Admiral, the poet Mary Fabilli, and the future film critic Pauline Kael, among others—who accepted him without criticizing his sexual life. He left Berkeley after two years, going East with his lover, who had a teaching job there, but it was necessary for the pair to take great precautions—not being seen together during the day, for example. Duncan was drafted and inducted into the army in 1941 but discharged very soon after that when he admitted to being homosexual.

"Toward the Shaman," one of Duncan's earliest works, embodies his anarchist principles. The poem, as he wrote William Everson, involves a revolution within the poet himself. It tells of personal suffering, poet and poem merging in a mutual expression.[12] Anarchism at this point supported a poetics of personal expression; poems, as Duncan said in his introduction to *The Years As Catches:*

ROBERT DUNCAN

First Poems (1939–1946), were a place where his "inner nature could reveal itself." [13] Certainly that inner nature had to withdraw before the prejudices of the world at large.

Duncan found at least a surface tolerance among libertarian and anarchist friends, but there was little toleration elsewhere. Homosexual communities did not offer an alternative, for they were, he felt, essentially cults, claiming a superior awareness or sensibility. In 1944, he published an essay entitled "The Homosexual in Society," attacking those who turn their sexual nature "into marketable oddities and sentimentalities." Following conventional anarchistic assumptions in claiming that no group or individual was superior to another, he called for a general human liberation in which each individual would be able to pursue his or her own identity. Duncan concluded that "one must disown *all* the special groups (nations, religions, sexes, races) that would claim allegiance" and work toward a general freedom and toleration. The essay was both idealistic and, for its time, radical.[14]

John Crowe Ransom had earlier accepted Duncan's poem "An African Elegy" for the *Kenyon Review,* but when he read "The Homosexual in Society," he withdrew his offer, saying the poem seemed to contain "obvious homosexual advertisement." [15] A correspondence followed that was restrained, for the most part even cordial, but in the end Ransom remained unconvinced by arguments that he had misread the poem, and it did not appear in his magazine.

ASPIRATIONS OF THE WORD

Read today, the poem seems less concerned with "homosexual advertisement" than with an appalling self-hatred. Duncan uses Africa as a metaphor for deep emotional conflict. The speaker identifies with Desdemona, but not in order to see Othello as a lover. At the poem's core, one finds a masochistic fantasy of self-destruction, a fantasy that is wholly within the jungle of the mind; as in "Toward the Shaman," the work is exceedingly private and inner, less concerned with homosexual desire than a desire for self-annihilation.

"An African Elegy" is important as an indication of the direction Duncan's poetics would follow in their erasure of the self and ultimate attention to language rather than ego. In the end, poetry as dictation would replace the early personal poems, but there is a clear psychological bond between them. Certainly one thing the later poetry was to attempt was the effacement of the poet.

Michael Davidson argued in *The San Francisco Renaissance* that Bay Area poetry in the 1940s was united by "faith in personal statement and confession." "Rhetoric, in the minds of the forties poets," he said, "was related not to figurative language or logic of argument but to the dramatic enhancement of subjective states."[16] Duncan's early works clearly fit that description; they are strongly personal and lyrical. The "Treesbank Poems," the opening poems in his first book, *Heavenly City, Earthly City* (1947), draw, for example, on romantic rhetoric—for example, in the lines

"You hunt / among the shadows of your life that haunt / sleep's depth...."[17]

In "An Apollonian Elegy" Duncan saw himself as an orphic, Apollonian poet, but the work itself is a romantic, Dionysian exercise in rhapsodic ecstacy. This is also true of the title poem, characterized largely by rhetorical ecstacies that poetry had generally abandoned long before. And yet some of the poems in the book have much force as personal statement—for example, "Among My Friends Love Is a Great Sorrow" and "I Am a Most Fleshly Man." These deal openly with Duncan's homosexuality, the first evoking the pathos of sexual difference (or "irregularity," as he called it in his introduction to *The Years as Catches*) and the second, in the tradition of troubadour lyric, attempting to charm a potential lover.

Pound's response to the book was "Why do you still have to go through that?"[18] But this was in fact a direction followed by many other poets around Duncan. Rexroth, for example, was self-consciously drawing on romantic poetics, effectively borrowing from Wordsworth in his own lyrical, often deeply elegiac works collected in *In What Hour* (1940), *The Phoenix and the Tortoise* (1944), and the most acclaimed of his early volumes, *The Signature of All Things* (1950). At this point in his career Duncan seemed altogether content in the company of Rexroth and others who found poetic authority within the self. But that soon changed. He originally shared, for example, the local admiration for Kenneth Patchen but then withdrew his

ASPIRATIONS OF THE WORD

enthusiasm "because Patchen's writing was self-indulgent, and didn't measure up." [19]

Perhaps the most important figure in Duncan's movement from a personal poet to one who drew his work from sources beyond the self, was H. D., the subject of a long discursive, meditative, and autobiographical work, "The H. D. Book," that Duncan began in 1960 but never completed. He had first encountered her early imagist work in high school, but it was the later poems that were to be the greater catalysts. He started reading passages from her *Trilogy* when they began to appear in 1944 and, with the publication of the final volume in 1946, placed her among his greatest luminaries. During World War II, she had become deeply involved with theosophy, but an interest in Hermeticism had developed much earlier—it was in fact evident in one of her earliest poems, "Hermes of the Ways." In *The Walls Do Not Fall*, the first book of her *Trilogy*, she wrote:

> Thoth, Hermes, the stylus
> the palette, the pen, the quill endure,
>
> though our books are a floor
> of smouldering ash under our feet.[20]

Fundamentally she was evoking here the Hermetic alchemical tradition, the capacity to make gold where there was only base metal. In *Trilogy,* London, destroyed by the

Germans, is alchemically transformed into poetry. the opening of *Tribute to the Angels,* H. D. invokes Hermes Trismegistus as the "patron of alchemists"—and poets. With his magic, the poet can use "fire and breathe" to "re-invoke, re-create / opal, onyx, obsidian, // now scattered in the shards / men tread upon."[21] This kind of transformation—beginning in conflict and war but concluding in art—would become fundamental to Duncan's own poetics. He would become an alchemist of words.

Strictly speaking, for Duncan, however, the alchemical act would not create something new but would return the imagination to older recognitions that dissention and war had tried to destroy. "Our work is to arouse in a contemporary consciousness," Duncan concluded, "reverberations of old myth, to prepare the ground so that when we return to read we will see our modern texts charged with a plot that had already begun before the first signs and signatures we have found worked upon the walls of Altamira or Pech-Merle" ("H. D. Book" I.3, 67).

Art in this sense was clearly not personal statement. H. D., wrote Duncan, saw the universe as a palimpsest, a series of writings and erasures, in which the divine was forever emergent and fugitive. One could find there the traces of the divine and clarify them again. In this interpretation Duncan defended a deeply Neoplatonic vision, one that was wholly different from Olson's. Duncan literally meant that poetry could locate a point of initiation prior to

ASPIRATIONS OF THE WORD

the self; that location, in fact, as *Trilogy* affirmed, was one of art's sacred tasks.

In the 1940s and 1950s, Duncan investigated various poetics that might show him a way out of the earlier lyrical expressive work like "An African Elegy." In the process, he tested possibilities that included formalist techniques and imitations of Stein, and the poetry of dictation, but none ultimately proved adequate except "Projective Verse"; in Olson he found one who could "open up everything I am."[22] He also discovered Levertov's "The Shifting" in an issue of *Origin* in 1952 and Creeley's *The Gold Diggers,* which he read in 1954. Together these works suggested a new artistic movement in which he could have a part. By the mid-1950s, he had shifted the direction of his own poetry, and by the spring of 1955 he was at work on the prologue to *Letters* and poems for *The Opening of the Field,* in which his commitment to Olson's poetics solidified. When Donald Allen edited *The New American Poetry* a few years later, Duncan "saw absolutely no meaning at all to being in something called San Francisco."[23] He would henceforth be identified primarily as part of the Black Mountain group.

But one must be careful not to attribute too much to Olson's influence. In "The H. D. Book" Duncan pointed out that in "Projective Verse," Olson gave primary emphasis to "the cosmic imperative of form over the psychic need for fulfillment or story," In fact, H. D. had in effect done this as well, as had Emerson and other writers in the Hermetic tradition generally. Duncan, furthermore, did not follow Olson in rejecting Western traditions for Mayan and Aztec civilization; like H. D., he drew heavily on the classical and Christian heritage, particularly Logos theology, in his work.

Like H. D., he found in Christianity analogies to his poetics: H. D., he said, returned "to the concept of the Christos as the incarnation of Helios, most real or only real in His manhood" ("H. D. Book" II.5, 83). The notion of poetry as incarnation is utterly essential in Duncan's poetics as well as H. D.'s, but it is very much contrary to the temper of the era. Europe had just survived two wars that had at least in some part been rooted in the belief that spiritual power could be manifest in an individual—whether the Emperor Franz Joseph, one of the last rulers to claim authority as a divine right, or Hitler, who claimed to embody the spirit of the *Volk*. The very notion of an individual invested with spiritual authority—a notion central to Christian history and studied by Duncan's Berkeley professor Ernst Kantorowicz in *The King's Two Bodies*—had been repudiated as a source for political authority. It was H. D.'s role in Duncan's professional growth to preserve the notion and demonstrate its continuing value for the poet. Basic to H. D.'s poetics was her Platonic, Gnostic view that the poet could be invested with the divine, "the cosmic imperative of form." For her and for Duncan, that cosmic imperative was no cold abstraction but Eros itself: "The Christ of Lawrence and H. D.," Duncan concluded,

ASPIRATIONS OF THE WORD

"is of the same order as the Helios or the crystal body of Aphrodite in Pound's cantos, or the Living God of Lawrence's last poems."[24]

Other analogies from Christian theology entered Duncan's poetics. For example, he saw the poet in a fundamentally priestly role. Just as the priest does not have to understand the sacrament he performs or even be in a state of grace to perform it, so the poet does not have to understand the poem he or she has written—or, for that matter, believe in what it says.

The poet closest to Duncan during the years he developed his concept of the poet as priest rather than true creator was Jack Spicer, whom he addressed in a letter in 1947 in the words Eliot had used to describe Pound: *il miglior fabbro,* the great craftsman.[25] When Duncan shifted his allegiance to Olson, he alienated Spicer, but with the publication of Spicer's *After Lorca* in 1957, he noted that Spicer had "taken his place again among my primaries."[26]

A decade earlier Duncan, Spicer, and Blaser had formed the core of a circle of poets, most of them homosexual, that met nightly at Duncan's quarters near the university in Berkeley. During a series of ten evenings that winter, Duncan wrote the sequence of poems titled *Medieval Scenes.* To begin each, he took one or more epigraphs; these served as the seed for the poem, which he then began to write without reflection or further thought. If he felt he had lost his way, he would stop and begin again. *Medieval Scenes* and other poems written soon after were in this sense "dictated"; the poet merely transcribed what he believed the poem called forth. The poem in this way had become "an event in language." The "divinity" that had made it possible, said Duncan, was "not a personal genius, but the genius of the language." [27]

Among themselves, the group that met at Hearst Street practiced "not touching"—not expressing sexual desire physically. In life as in the work, the poet was to efface himself or herself; the only focus was the process of composition. The result was Platonic, a reaching toward and, in the poem itself, possession of ideal form.

Emerson provided epigraphs for four of the poems in *Medieval Scenes*.[28] Of these, the most telling in the context of Duncan's poetics is the epigraph from "Experience" with which "The Helmet of Goliath" begins: "Souls never touch their objects. An innavigable sea washes with silent waves between us and the things we aim at and converse with."[29] Emerson gives as an example the death of his child two years earlier, leaving him with such a strong sense of estrangement from the world that only death itself seemed absolute and real. "The Helmet of Goliath" concerns "not touching" and the estrangement it implies. In the poem, men are seated around a table, each isolated from the others, "[grieving] / grief can teach them nothing / nor can they touching touch" (*MS,* not paginated); but in the "darkened helmet" of Goliath, each poet's "curious" face can be seen. The helmet itself—not the poet who wears it—is said to sing.

ASPIRATIONS OF THE WORD

Goliath was slain by the boy David, who was a lyric poet. The poet who wears the helmet can neither grieve nor sing; he can not feel. But he participates, or at least is present, in the creation of poetry. He is like Emerson, who could no longer feel but whose words proposed the poem. He is also like Orpheus (with whom Spicer in particular identified), whose songs, following the loss of Eurydice, were dictated by Apollo. Orpheus lost Eurydice before he became the singer of Apollo's songs; Emerson lost his son; the men around the table in Duncan's house remain isolated from each other. In each case, loss is where poems began, but they are not lyric poems. "The speech of poets seems to deny / all love," Duncan wrote. "They listen to forbidden music" (*MS,* not paginated).

A month later, in March, 1947, Duncan, however, wrote his "Ode for Dick Brown," which calls for renewal and fulfillment through sexuality, and the following year he wrote "The Venice Poem," his first major work, which makes a similar claim. "The Venice Poem" was, Duncan said, the first in which "I had both known what I had to do—something more in writing than knowing what you *want* to do—and known as I worked that I was able to do it." [30] The poem was then "an event in language," but it was also very personal.

"The Venice Poem" is an instance of what Pound called "melopoeia," poetry that is organized by "some musical property." [31] Duncan's ideas about musical process and form were drawn from Igor Stravinsky, whose book of lectures on musical form, *The Poetics of Music,* he had recently reviewed for the Berkeley undergraduate literary magazine, *Occident.* In this book, Stravinsky argued that music was derived not from nature but from artifice and was ruled by "principle" rather than "self-expression."[32] He argued, that is, for a classical approach to composition. "The Venice Poem" has a conventional sonata structure, with three parts plus a coda. Within that form the poem was composed "in the sequence of the musical phrase," following "the tone leading of vowels," as Pound had suggested.[33] The outer shell of the structure was formal and restrictive, but within, the poem moved according to its own musical intentions.

This poem had roots in the failure of one of Duncan's love affairs. Had it been written a few years earlier, it might have become another of the "Treesbank Poems." Indeed it may be to those poems that Duncan is referring when he says that in the discovery of sexual betrayal, poetry does not exist, and "the words in the dark go round and round."[34] The poet is trapped in his solipsistic woe, and the poem becomes "doggerel" (*SP,* 68).

Venice, the poem recalls, is the city of Venus, where stone lions seem suppliant to the phallic bell tower that rises over San Marco. It is also a city of deceptions, the city of Iago in Shakespeare's *Othello.* Such deceptions, the poem claims, are produced not by the poet but by the city. The poet is an innocent in a devious city that reveals its nature in the music of the bell tower, celebrating the ultimate

ASPIRATIONS OF THE WORD

power of sexuality. Venice and its people seem figures in a sexual dreamscape: St. Mark's is described as a configuration of domes, Iago is compared to an angel (homosexual parlance for "lover"), and Duncan (as earlier in "An African Elegy") sees himself in the masochistic role of Desdemona; the poet's "heart [thirsts] after ... [the city's] fountains" (*SP,* 47). But this city of desire is also a city of betrayal. To avoid the anguish that comes to those who are betrayed, the poet must be "driven by the language itself" (*SP,* 70); he must move according to the imperatives of the words rather than personal needs. The city itself speaks through the poem, and in this voice the poem celebrates both sexual betrayal and sexual ecstasy. The poem ends with the exaltation of all sexual feeling, including even the "pain, anger, and endurance" it entails. The bell tower is seen at the end as the type of all "fatherly towers in the air" (*SP,* 76).

Duncan said that the last section of the poem told him "that Hell was the womb of Heaven; that the extreme passion of painful experience of love in conflict was the formation of a passage in feeling in which a new self was to be born" (*CG,* ix). That recognition has affinities with H.D.'s alchemical poetics, whereby the perfected work can be wrought out of the ruins of war.

Caesar's Gate, a collection of poems written in 1949 and 1950, pursues that notion further. In a preface completed many years after he wrote the poems, Duncan stated that he understood "Caesar's Gate" as the entrance to "a realm of sodomitic empire claim in love," but that very realm is identified in "The Second Night in the Week" as a wasteland (*CG,* xi). The irony is certain, much like the emotional sterility in "The Helmet of Goliath," which is a prerequisite to the poem. "Poetry," Duncan wrote, "is the very life of the soul: the body's discovery that it can dream."[35] But the dream itself, it is clear, may well begin in aridity or anguish.

In *Derivations,* which includes poems written between 1950 and 1956, one finds Duncan searching for authority, submitting to it, and transforming it into something characteristically his own. His principal forebears in that volume are Gertrude Stein and Olson. The "Stein Imitations," which occupied Duncan early in the 1950s, grew from a fascination with Stein's work that he decided to pursue "blindly" until its appeal had been exhausted. Stein had considerable interest for Creeley, as we have seen (she was yet another on the list of authors that Olson wanted excluded from the Black Mountain curriculum), but it was the theoretical implications of her work that attracted him. Duncan was particularly interested in her mannerisms and distinctive sound, especially her use of verbals and repetition. He came perhaps as close as anyone could to duplicating her style. One wonders if Stein herself would, at some points, have been able to distinguish the original from the imitation.

In the Stein imitations, Duncan set out in effect to eradicate his own presence. As in *Medieval Scenes,* he took an extreme position in denying the poet's presence in the poem. He had thought the imitations would show him exactly where he was *not* Stein,[36] but in some passages, he seemingly eradicated his presence altogether, implying that a poem can lie very much outside the poet. Many years later, when that position was argued by Barrett Watten, Duncan, as noted earlier, strongly objected, although Watten could have found support for his argument in Duncan's own work.

Jayne L. Walker argued that in the Stein imitations "associations of sound and rhythm . . . subvert and resist rational ordering."[37] Like "The Venice Poem," the Stein imitations follow "the tone leading of the vowels"; musical structure, rather than ideas, are in control. Stein had been interested in the semantic transformations that subtle changes in cadence and syntax can effect, and for this reason, her work has always been important for writers perfecting their craft. But those transformations take place within her very mannered style, and if Duncan was going to make any original contribution as a poet, he had to find his own stylistic conditions.

The conditions he found are announced in the poem he placed first in *Derivations,* "An Essay at War," in which he views the Korean conflict as an analogy to the making of poems. In "The Venice Poem" he proposed "Hell" as "the womb of Heaven." In "An Essay at War" he asserted that "we are always at war."[38] The good necessarily must be rooted in conflict and chaos. The poem is itself a battlefield, whose resolution is the dance of language.[39] Behind that declaration, one may speculate, is not only the example of H. D. but also the Hermetic doctrine which considers the world as fallen and irremediably evil. From there, the individual and by extension the poem struggle upward to harmony and light. Duncan's poetics entail an unrelentingly search for moments of transfiguration when "the language takes fire" (*Derivations,* 12). It is a poetics of aspiration, drawing on a desire for transcendence.

In "An Essay at War," Duncan proposed that his poetry become "a proposition / in movement" (*Derivations,* 9). Stein too was concerned with movement, but her solutions were in the particulars of her style, and anyone who adopts them—for example, using verbals rather than concrete nouns—necessarily sounds like her. To devise his "proposition / in movement," Duncan needed another master, and that is what he found in Olson. Stein's solutions depended heavily on technique; in "Projective Verse," on the other hand, Olson limited himself to much more general solutions. He said, for example, that "always one perception must must must MOVE, INSTANTER, ON ANOTHER!"[40] He then left the poet to work out his or her own means of doing that effectively and smoothly.

The initial effect the essay had on Duncan can be found in *Letters,* originally published as a separate book but then included as the final section of *Derivations.* In the preface to *Letters,* Duncan identifies the poem as "a designd

ASPIRATIONS OF THE WORD

feeling" that the poet is compelled to write out of "an intensity of excitement" (*Derivations,* 89). In place of the classical restraint of "The Venice Poem," the mannered verse of the Stein imitations, the rhapsodic diction of the early poems, and the various other poetic styles and methods Duncan had earlier pursued, there is here a progressive speech in which one word aspires after the next—a true "proposition / in movement." Language is drawn forward most fundamentally not by meter, and certainly not by the desire to formulate a particular idea, but by cadence, modulation in sound (moving, for example, from long to short vowels as the poem reaches ecstatic awareness), and meticulous attention to line breaks. This would be Duncan's final mode and his greatest:

> :   in
> s p i r e d / the aspirate
> the aspirant almost
> without breath
> it is a breath out
> breathed—an aspiration
> pictured as the familiar spirit
> hovered
> above
> each loved one[.]
>
> (*Derivations,* 94)

ROBERT DUNCAN

Vowels, Duncan wrote, are "physical corridors of the imagination emitting passionately breaths of flame" and give "aweful intimations of eternal life," while consonants "confine the spirit to articulations of space and time." The poem is then a struggle between limitlessness and confinement, ecstacy and restraint, but it aspires to the freedom of vowels, and it is vowels that are ultimately triumphant. Duncan's works are orchestrations of sound moving from confinement to joy. "In a poem," he wrote, "the vowels appear like the flutterings of an owl caught in a web," and "the joy / is a great scuttering of feathers words" (*Derivations,* 132, 143). Heard in the manner Duncan wished, his lines, whatever their value as statement, are struggles toward the freedom of vowels, as in the conclusion of "The Propositions," where he adjures the poet to

> move into the Dance   Whose bonds men hold
>   holy   :   the Light

life lights in like eyes.[41]

Duncan's essay "The Truth and Life of Myth" is as important to his work, particularly *The Opening of the Fields,* his first major book, as "Human Universe" is to Olson's. Both essays are considerations of poetics in social and moral terms. Duncan names Cassirer and Freud (whom he identifies as a mythologist rather than psychologist) as

ASPIRATIONS OF THE WORD

sources for his work together with "the mythopoeic weavings of Pound's *Cantos* in which 'all ages are contemporaneous.' " Cassirer's attention to language as a symbolic act, Freud's literary rendering of the subconscious, and Pound's creation of an epic history-mythology may have been less important to Duncan, however, than the fourth source he named: "Jane Harrison's definition of the dithyramb as 'the song that makes Zeus leap or beget' " (*FC,* 6). Harrison, one of the Cambridge Ritualists, believed that the dithyramb had its origins in a ritual dance through which a male initiate believed he could transform himself, in imagination, into a god. In this dance an adolescent male declared his freedom from women and in particular from his mother—an especially significant point, one would guess, for Duncan, who had begun to see his adopted mother as the sinister and domineering figure he would describe in the poem "My Mother Would Be A Falconress." In the dance, the adolescent could be suffused with the spirit of the god Dionysus—could in fact become an incarnation of the god. Although it was Dionysus whose spirit entered through the dance, it was understood to be Zeus as well—or, rather, Dionysus was viewed as simply a youthful manifestation of the greater god.[42] To create a song that would make "Zeus leap or beget" was, therefore, to incarnate the god in the poem—and in oneself insofar as one made the words one's own in reading them. "The Word is for me," Duncan concluded, "living Flesh" (*FC,* 15).

ROBERT DUNCAN

Duncan went on to list three forces that "move to incarnate themselves in the poem" (although, he added, he could as well name two or seven or seventy-two): "the words," "the life experience and imagination of the poet," and "the actual body of the poet" (*FC,* 18). If the Stein imitations tended to efface the writer from the poetry, Duncan's later work insists on the poet as present in the words. This is not to say that the poem fulfills a personal need or that it is an expression of ego; it is rather that the language achieves its force by drawing on the poet's sensibility, emotion, imagination, and experience.

Olson had argued similarly in "Projective Verse," insisting that the work embody the poet's rhythms, understood as inseparable from his or her breath and emotional and sexual being. It was not the business of the poet to mimetically represent the exterior world or to testify in some neutral capacity to what was "real," but to speak from within the self, within "his nature as he is participant in the large force." The poet who remained within the self, Olson concluded, would "be able to listen, and his hearing through himself will give him secrets objects share."[43] "The Truth and Life of Myth" opens with an epigraph from Harrison's *Themis,* in which she identifies myth as "the arrangement of the incidents"—not the incidents themselves but their pattern, which is abstract and felt rather than concrete and nameable. Myth, wrote Duncan, "is the story of what cannot be told," which he compared to "the mystic gnosis"

ASPIRATIONS OF THE WORD

of Theosophy, a secret knowledge (like, for example, the names Stein created in *Tender Buttons*). To create the poem, the writer had to be an adept, participating in its dithyrambic dance, or rather a "myth-teller," reciting not "a story of what he thinks or wishes life to be" but "the story that *comes to him* and forces his telling" (*FC,* 1).

The Opening of the Field (1960) begins with "Often I Am Permitted To Return To A Meadow," which has its roots in one of Duncan's recurrent dreams (a "story that *comes to him*"). In the meadow, which Duncan sees as his "place of first permission," children dance a "ring a round of roses," the medieval dance that was supposed to keep out the plague but always ends in death—"we all fall down." Beneath the meadow is the "Lady," Kore or Persephone, queen of the underworld and goddess of spring. Kore and Dionysus, Harrison argued, were both late versions of the earth goddess or Great Mother (hence the androgenous nature of Dionysus). The dithyramb called Dionysus into being, brought him up, like Kore in the spring, into the light; and the children's dance can be seen as a way of invoking him. The grass is, like Whitman's leaves of grass and like Dionysus, a source of life. The grass comes from the world of Kore and Dionysus and points east away from the sun; in so doing, it turns away from Apollo. The implication is that this poetry is not Apollonian—a poetry of pure but static form, denying change—but Dionysian, a poetry of "a proposition / in movement." But although it is presently alive in its cadences and musical modulations, it also is doomed like victims of the plague.

This is a pure instance of Duncan's fatalism; the sun, it is said, will set in an hour, and the dance is no more than an hour's reprieve from catastrophe. But in that reprieve, there is opportunity for transfiguration and transcendence: "In the feet that measure the dance of my pages," wrote Duncan in "The Structure of Rime I," "I hear cosmic intoxications of the man I will be" (*OF,* 12).

Transfiguration is possible in part because of "rime," that network of correspondences—or "absolute scale of resemblance and disresemblance," as Duncan called it in "The Structure of Rime II"—that holds the universe together. The dance is directed by the "Master of Rime," and one can move only as he permits, but the one who is obedient can find the links or correspondences, the rimes that allow one to pass from one point or recognition into another. The eternal transformations of the universe are not haphazard or confused; they have their harmony, which in turn has its correspondence in the musical evolution of the poem.[44]

Perhaps the book's most frequently anthologized work is "A Poem Beginning With A Line By Pindar." Reading the first Pythian Ode late at night, Duncan heard the third line—"The light foot hears you and the brightness begins"—as an evocation of a Dionysian dance. The words *light foot* suggested poetic meter, as if to say the dance was

ASPIRATIONS OF THE WORD

both the one in the meadow and the one in the language. "Immediately," wrote Duncan, "sight of Goya's great canvas [of Psyche seeing Cupid for the first time] . . . came to me, like a wave." Cupid seemed to him "the primal Eros" and Psyche "the First Soul" (*FC,* 17). Psyche had been forbidden to look at Cupid, and now, to be with him again, she had to submit to a series of extraordinary tasks. Her submission to those tasks is like the poet's submission to language and the Master of Rime, a submission that leads to a transfigurative view of beauty.

The poem traces the importance of submission and the failure of the public world at present to provide leaders worthy of being submitted to. The key to success, for the poet as for Psyche, is "*the mystery of Love.*" Near the end of the poem, Duncan lists three mountains, each associated with a form of love: "Mount Segur," where the Gnostic Cathars chose to be destroyed rather than submit to the Papal armies; "Mount Victoire," the mountain in Provence with which Cézanne fused his identity in his paintings; and "Mount Tamalpais," the mountain north of San Francisco that rises above Stinson Beach, where Duncan and his lover were living when the poem was written. These three mountains are an instance of rime. There is no geographic or historical connection among them, but they share associations with a transfigurative love, the intimate identification of self and object that sent Psyche in search of Cupid and that Duncan considered the source of art.

ROBERT DUNCAN

Roots and Branches (1964) is actually two books, *Roots and Branches (1959–60),* and *Windings (1961–63).* Like *Derivations,* they consist largely of Duncan's attempt to find other poetic voices through which he can speak—a project very much like one Spicer had been pursuing in such books as *After Lorca* (1957). Now in *Roots and Branches,* Duncan conjured up the voices of Shelley, Baudelaire, Dante, and H. D., among others. In this work Duncan again assumes the role of the medium. *Roots and Branches,* perhaps his most explicitly theosophical work, includes his play *Adam's Way: A Play Upon Theosophical Themes* and his reminiscences of coincidences in his own life that a Theosophist would interpret as signs of the spiritual realm at work in the world. "A Sequence of Poem's for H. D.'s Birthday" includes an account of a visit to a medium who told him that Duncan that his mother was in the room with them, though his mother was, he believed, at that time thousands of miles away. If ever a medium were a fraud, it would seem, it was this one. But then he realized the third presence in the room could have been his true mother. In another autobiographical piece, "Two Presentations," he noted that he was originally named for his biological father, Edward Howard Duncan, and that when his foster parents renamed him Robert Edward Symmes, the name Howard was "lost." Then, riding on the Union-Howard bus, he heard a schoolgirl's voice breaking through his concentration and dictating "fragments of a message

ASPIRATIONS OF THE WORD

that seemd meant for me and at the same time to direct the poem" that he was writing (*RB,* 74).

As these phenomena demonstrate, things that seem coincidental may operate on another level. Thus Duncan felt that his "H. D. Book" had in some way cost his adoptive mother her life. In one sense it did: H. D. as a creative force had replaced her in the maternal role; through H. D. he found his imaginative life in poetry.

Duncan's works may at first seem a field of unrelated references, but these references soon reveal deep correspondences or rimes with each other. The divisions between the inner self and the world at large fade. The monarch butterfly in "Roots and Branches," for example, "[awakens] transports of an inner view of things" (*RB,* 3). Externality is a map of another world if, like the Theosophist, one is attuned to the webs of rime.

In "After Reading H. D.'s *Hermetic Definitions,*" Duncan noted that H. D., reading St.-John Perse, mistook the word *quantième* for *quatrième*. The music and meaning in the poem consequently shifted, resulting not in something wrong, but merely in something different from what Perse wrote. Duncan is not issuing an invitation to randomness; there still must be patterns to follow. One must still be obedient to the task, must submit to necessity. The objective is not to please oneself: the poet's work, like the work of the medium, exists ultimately for others. The poet, says Duncan, "writes instinctively, like bees," and however his work may transfigure himself, he "serves the life of the hive" (*RB,* 83).

"Structure of Rime XX" is one of the darkest poems Duncan wrote about the poet's task. Here the Master of Rime instructs the poet "to lose heart." The encounter with void or absence is part of the poet's task, "for the pit of despair wants you to come there," says the Master. At that point the poet does despair, but there is no comfort from the Master, who smiles and leaves him in solitude.

Bending the Bow (1968) has two major and opposed centers: on the one hand, Vietnam and the strife it bred at home and, on the other, poetry as a passage to transcendence. The book's introduction begins as a Jeremiad, speaking of the present as "the last days of our own history" and suggesting that there is no political course out of "the form to which we now belong."[45] Among other things, Duncan rejects the kind of communal and utopian thinking that was then common in the counterculture and that other poets, like Rexroth and Gary Snyder, were defending.

But then Duncan turns to poetry as "the ever forming of bodies in language in which breath moves." Poetry, in short, is the redemptive agent in a shattered history (*BB,* ii). Nonetheless, a poem is not free of the strife and conflicts that make a Vietnam; "long before this war," he says, he saw "wrath move in the music that troubles me" (*BB,* iii). Poem and poet are no more free of the furors of war than are governments, and Duncan therefore advises himself to

ASPIRATIONS OF THE WORD

avoid the error of the self-righteous who were was all around him.

Hermes, says Duncan, created both "the bow and the lyre to confound Apollo, god of poetry." The bow is necessary in order that the lyre can make music, but it is also a weapon of war. Poetry is not a privileged field, an Arcadia free of conflict, and words are not to create airy illusions. Poetry is rather an act of naming, bringing the universe, the "*grand collage,* I name it" into being: "The gnostics and magicians claim to know or would know Its real nature, which they believe to be miswritten or cryptically written in the text of the actual world. But Williams is right in his *no ideas but in things*; for It has only the actual universe in which to realize Itself" (*BB,* ix). In insisting that the universe named in language is not just a construction, Duncan was opposing his own work to the ideas of the structuralists, among other theorists, who were making great forays into the universities at this time. The poem articulated the absolutely real—that was the reason for submission: behind the poet in creating the poem was "my immediate Creator" (*BB,* viii).

In his *Imaginary Elegies,* Spicer had charged the poet to "Be like God," a charge taken with utter seriousness in the Spicer/Duncan/Blaser circle, and here Duncan reiterates the essentially divine, creative function the poet performs. But he does so by being, in priestly fashion, thoroughly obedient to the poem and the universe as it is rather than to any personal desire or necessity. Nor is there a matter of pleasure or personal satisfaction: at "the living center . . . there is no composure but a life-spring of dissatisfaction in all orders from which the restless ordering of our poetry comes" (*BB,* x). Vietnam, by implication, is not a subject for protest but the material out of which poems can rise. In its form and sound, its very construction, the work participates in war. "Bending the Bow" speaks of bringing Hermes' bow back "till the end rimes in the taut string / with the sending"; the arrow that kills has the grace of the song that delights (*BB,* 7).

Poetry for Duncan was never to be used, as Denise Levertov was then using it, fundamentally as a platform for protest. "Poetry is a contagion," Duncan said in "Shadows." In "Orders," he identified the "rage, grief, dismay" in Schubert's "poetry" as "transports of beauty." Perhaps the most horrific recognition of this sort is Duncan's admission of his own pleasure in giving pain; in "My Mother Would Be A Falconress," one of the poems for which he is best known, he sees himself as a falcon trained by his mother to destroy other birds, but then he turns on her, pecking with his beak at her wrist. He has learned the pleasure of drawing blood.

Bending the Bow introduces a new sequence, "Passages." The title is the subject of "Structure of Rime XXIII": "No matter how many times the cards are handled and laid out to lay out their plan of the future—a fortune—only passages of what is happening" (*BB,* 23). The cards,

ASPIRATIONS OF THE WORD

like words, can be set in a seemingly infinite number of orders, and each of those orders could in some circumstance be true. Duncan next says that he would "give . . . an illusion of grieving" and then that he would "give . . . an illusion of not grieving" (*BB,* 23).

Each passage, like each fortune, has its stable truth, but what matters in the poem, as in the telling of a fortune, is the telling itself, the ways in which data are arranged; as Harrison said, myth is "the arrangement of the incidents." "The Fire   Passages 13" begins and ends with words, like the following, printed separately from each other so as to emphasize their simplicity and clarity:

jump	stone	hand	leaf	shadow	sun
day	plash	coin	light	downstream	fish[.]

(*BB,* 40)

Placed this way, the words give "a dawn-of-man scene," or childhood scene, as Duncan wrote in "The Truth and Life of Myth" (*FC,*) These provide a frame within which he contrasts two paintings and two corresponding sensibilities. One painting is Piero di Cosimo's *A Forest Fire,* a transcendent vision of harmony; the other, *Christ Bearing the Cross,* by Hieronymus Bosch, is a vision of utter corruption. This corruption is then likened to the deceptions and malevolence of politicians like Nixon and Goldwater, the catastrophe of nuclear arsenals, and the continuing corrosion of American cities. Duncan quotes Whitman, pointing to bureaucrats, clerks and politicians who use the nation to satisfy their own needs and whose "cherished secret scheme is to dissolve the union of these states" (*BB,* 44). By contrast, Duncan offers the Hermetic philosopher Marsilio Ficino, who describes music as both a product of the self and a source of its harmony. The corrupt and the transcendent exist in an equilibrium, both of them part of a grand mosaic.

Following the publication of *Bending the Bow* in 1968, Duncan did not publish another major book until *Ground Work: Before the War* in 1984. Individual poems appeared separately (for example, the group of five "Passages," which appeared in a volume entitled *Tribunals* in 1970), but these were not intended for broad circulation. Spicer, several years before, had made an even greater withdrawal, insisting that his work not be circulated outside San Francisco and enclosing himself in a circle of people, primarily poets, who followed the course of his work attentively. By making a similar decision, Duncan stressed the importance of the poem over whatever critics might make of it. Olson had to some degree suffered by becoming the center of a following as interested at times in his politics as in his poetry. Rexroth was a more extreme example of the dangers of being a public figure: he was appearing at antiwar rallies dressed as a hippie and even writing a book on communes.

ASPIRATIONS OF THE WORD

Ground Work: Before the War and Duncan's last book, *Ground Work II: In the Dark* (published in 1987, the year before his death), include some of his most difficult poetry. Much of it begins in the work of other poets including Paul Celan, George Herbert, Ben Jonson, Rumi, Dante, and many others: "What works in me," Duncan says in "Illustrative Lines," "is not mine but / ancient survivals."[46] The books also include further poems from "Passages" and "Structures of Rime" interwoven with new sequences such as the "Dante Études" and "To Master Baudelaire," which can be read as an extension of the ground he had explored in earlier Baudelaire imitations. These books thus intensify the complexity of Duncan's field of operation, keeping ever more things in motion. As had been true since *Letters,* here too the poet always aspires to further and greater recognitions, moving up from chaos through language to transcendent insight:

> We pretend to speak.   The language is not ours and we move upward beyond our powers into
>
> words again   beyond us   unsure measures
>
> the poetry of the cosmos[.]
>
> (*GW*, 21)

Great attention is given to prosodic detail. *Ground Work* focuses on such matters as the fact that a caesura space is not "just an articulation of phrasings but a phrase itself of silence" (*GW,* ix). Words are set on the page with mathematical inflexibility. To avoid the kind of misprints that occurred in earlier books, *Ground Work: Before the War* was printed from a typescript prepared directly under Duncan's supervision.

The general terms of Duncan's perspective remain as they were. The world is violent and fallen: in "Fragments of an Albigensian Rime," "the blood ran down" (*GW,* 50), and Duncan endures as "a predator of the marvelous." As the preface to *Bending the Bow* insisted, poetry had to remain true to the real, and so Duncan found himself drawn to the "darker reaches of a Silence / to which our symphonies refer" (*GW,* 92). In "After a Long Illness," the poem that closes *Ground Work II: In the Dark* and was apparently the last Duncan wrote, he says, "In the real I have always known myself" (*GWII,* 90). But "the real" is not defined in terms of the world at large; it is "the absolute Stillness" (*GWII,* 90).

Duncan's work revealed itself at the end as essentially stoic, indicating that the ultimate condition is not the Hermetic paradise of spirits and light but "an eternal arrest" (*GWII,* 90). The Master of Rime, not the Hermetic Brotherhood, opened the way to the void and the submission it requires.

ASPIRATIONS OF THE WORD

Notes

1. Robert Duncan, *Fictive Certainties* (New York: New Directions, 1985) 65. Further references will be noted parenthetically in the text as *FC*.

2. Duncan, "Returning to *Les Chimères* of Gérard de Nerval," *Audit* 4 (1967): 48–49.

3. Duncan, *Ground Work: Before the War* (New York: New Directions, 1984), 70–93. Further references will be noted parenthetically in the text as *GW*.

4. Duncan, *Roots and Branches* (New York: New Directions, 1968) 39. Further references will be noted parenthetically in the text as *RB*.

5. "The H. D. Book," book I, chapter 3, *Tri-Quarterly* 12 (Spring 1968): 80. Further references will be noted parenthetically in the text.

6. Duncan, "The H. D. Book," book I, chapter 5, *Stony Brook* 1/2 (Fall 1968): 12. Further references will be noted parenthetically in the text.

7. Charles Olson, *Human Universe and Other Essays* (New York, Grove, 1967) 67.

8. Olson, 59.

9. Ralph Waldo Emerson, *Conduct of Life* (Boston and New York: Houghton, Mifflin, 1883) 51.

10. Duncan, "Warp and Woof: Notes from a Talk," *Talking Poetics from Naropa Institute,* ed. Anne Waldman and Marilyn Webb (Boulder and London: Shambhala, 1978) vol. 1, 9.

11. H. D. and Duncan, *A Great Admiration: H. D./Robert Duncan Correspondence 1950–1961* (Venice, Calif.: Lapis, 1992) 36.

12. Duncan, "'Where as Giant Kings We Gatherd': Some Letters from Robert Duncan to William Everson, 1940 and After," *Sagetrieb* 4 (Fall/Winter 1985): 152–53.

13. Duncan, *The Years as Catches: First Poems (1939–1946)* (Berkeley: Oyez, 1966) i.

14. Duncan, "The Homosexual in Society," *Politics* 1 (August 1944): 209, 211.

15. Ekbert Faas, *Young Robert Duncan: Portrait of the Poet as Homosexual in Society* (Santa Barbara, Calif.: Black Sparrow Press, 1983) 151.

16. Michael Davidson, *The San Francisco Renaissance: Politics and Community at Mid-Century* (Cambridge [England] and New York: Cambridge University Press, 1989) 36.

17. Duncan, *Heavenly City, Earthly City* (Berkeley: Bern Porter, 1947) 4.

18. Reported in Michael André Bernstein and Burton Hatlen, "Interview with Robert Duncan," *Sagetrieb* 4 (Fall/Winter 1985): 91.

19. Bernstein and Hatlen, 105.

20. H. D., *Trilogy* (New York: New Directions, 1973) 16.

21. H. D., 63.

22. Quoted in Allen Ginsberg, *Allen Verbatim: Lectures on Poetry, Politics, Consciousness,* ed. Gordon Ball (New York: McGraw-Hill, 1974) 133.

23. Duncan and Michael McClure, "In Interview," *Conjunctions* 7 (1985): 84.

24. Duncan "The H. D. Book," book II, chapter 10, *Ironwood* 22 (1983): 58.

25. Faas, 221.

ASPIRATIONS OF THE WORD

26. From Duncan's autobiographical statement in *The New American Poetry: 1945–1960,* ed. Donald M. Allen (New York: Grove, 1960) 434.

27. Robin Blaser, "A Backward Glance," in Jack Spicer, *Collected Books* (Los Angeles, CA: Black Sparrow, 1975) 362.

28. *Medieval Scenes* has never been published as originally written, but versions published in 1950 and 1959 are gathered in Duncan, *Medieval Scenes: 1950 and 1959* (Kent, Ohio: Kent State University Libraries, 1978).

Ralph Waldo Emerson, *Essays: Second Series* (Boston and New York: Houghton, Mifflin, 1883) 52.

30. Duncan, *Caesar's Gate: Poems 1949–50* (Berkeley, Calif.: Sand Dollar, 1972) ix. Further references will be noted parenthetically in the text as *CG*.

31. Ezra Pound, *Literary Essays* (New York: New Directions, 1968) 25.

32. Duncan, "The Poetics of Music: Stravinsky," *Occident* (Spring 1948): 53.

33. Pound, 5; Faas, 260.

34. Duncan, *Selected Poems* (San Francisco: City Lights, 1959) 69. Further references will be noted in the text as *SP*.

35. Duncan, "Pages from a Notebook," in *The New American Poetry: 1945–1960,* ed. Donald M. Allen (New York: Grove, 1960) 401.

36. Bernstein and Hatlen, 120.

37. Jayne L. Walker, "Exercises in Disorder: Duncan's Imitations of Gertrude Stein," in *Scales of the Marvelous,* ed. Robert J. Bertholf and Ian W. Reid (New York: New Directions, 1979) 28.

ROBERT DUNCAN

38. Duncan, *Derivations: Selected Poems 1950–1956* (London: Fulcrum, 1968) 13. Further references will be noted parenthetically in the text as *SP*.

39. In my discussion of Duncan's poetics I am indebted to Nathaniel Mackey, *Gassire's Lute: Robert Duncan's Vietnam War Poems,* published serially in *Talisman: A Journal of Contemporary Poetry and Poetics* 5 (Fall 1990): 86–99; 6 (Spring 1991): 141–64; 7 (Fall 1991): 141–66; 8 (Spring 1992): 189–221. This is the essential book for any future consideration of Duncan's poetics.

40. Olson, 53.

41. Duncan, *The Opening of the Field* (New York: Grove, 1960) 37. Further references will be noted parenthetically in the text as *OF*.

42. See Jane Harrison, *Prolegomena to the Study of Greek Religion* (Cambridge [England]: Cambridge University Press, 1903); *Themis: A Study of the Social Origins of Greek Religion* (Cambridge [England]: Cambridge University Press, 1912).

43. Olson, 60.

44. This theme repeatedly emerges in the sequence; see, for example, "The Structure of Rime XIII" (*OF,* 83).

45. Duncan, *Bending the Bow* (New York: New Directions, 1968) i. Further references will be noted parenthetically in the text as *BB*.

46. Duncan, *Ground Work II: In the Dark* (New York: New Directions, 1987) 87. Further references will be noted parenthetically in the text as *GWII*.

SELECT BIBLIOGRAPHY

General Works

Books

Conte, Joseph M. *Unending Design: The Forms of Postmodern Poetry.* Ithaca: Cornell University Press, 1991. Important discussions of formal structures in Creeley and Duncan; less attention to Olson.

Dawson, Fielding. *The Black Mountain Book.* New ed. Rocky Mount, N.C.: North Carolina Wesleyan College Press, 1991. Memoir.

Duberman, Martin. *Black Mountain: A Study in Community.* New York: Dutton, 1972. Interpretive history of the college.

Faas, Ekbert. *Towards a New American Poetics: Essays and Interviews.* Santa Barbara, Calif.: Black Sparrow Press, 1979. Interviews with Creeley, Duncan, and Olson.

Harris, Mary Emma. *The Arts at Black Mountain College.* Cambridge, Mass.: MIT Press, 1987. Detailed history with emphasis on the visual arts but with consideration of poetry community under Olson.

Lane, Mervin, ed. *Black Mountain: Sprouted Seeds: An Anthology of Personal Accounts.* Knoxville: University of Tennessee Press, 1990. Reminiscences and commentary on the college by faculty, students, and others associated with the school.

Works by Robert Creeley

Books

Le Fou. Columbus, Ohio: Golden Goose Press, 1952.
The Kind of Act Of. Palma de Mallorca: Divers Press, 1953.
The Immoral Proposition. Karlsruhe-Durlach, Germany, and Highlands, N.C.: Jonathan Williams, 1953.
The Gold Diggers. Palma de Mallorca: Divers Press, 1954; new edition, *The Gold Diggers and Other Stories.* New York: Scribner's, 1965; London: Calder, 1965.
A Snarling Garland of Christmas Verse. Palma de Mallorca: Divers Press, 1954.
All That Is Lovely in Men. Asheville, N.C.: Jonathan Williams, 1955.
If You. San Francisco: Porpoise Bookshop, 1956.
The Whip. Worcester, England: Migrant Books, 1957.
A Form of Woman. New York: Jargon Books, 1959.
For Love: Poems 1950–1960. New York: Scribner's, 1962.
The Island. New York: Scribner's, 1963; London: Calder, 1964.
Words. Rochester, Mich.: Perishable Press, 1965; New York: Scribner's, 1967.

SELECT BIBLIOGRAPHY

About Women. Los Angeles: Gemini, 1966.
Poems 1950–1965. London: Calder and Boyars, 1966.
The Finger. Los Angeles: Black Sparrow Press, 1968.
NUMBERS: A Sequence to Robert Indiana. New York: Poets Press, 1968.
The Charm: Early and Uncollected Poems. Madison, Wis.: Perishable Press, 1967; London: Calder and Boyers, 1971.
Divisions & Other Early Poems. Mt. Horeb, Wis.: Perishable Press, 1968.
Pieces. Los Angeles: Black Sparow Press, 1968; New York: Scribner's, 1969.
Mazatlan: Sea. San Francicso: Poets Press, 1969.
Hero. New York: Indianakatz, 1969.
A Quick Graph: Collected Notes & Essays. San Francisco: Four Seasons, 1970.
Mary's Fancy. New York: Bouwerie Editions, 1970.
In London. Bolinas, Calif.: Angel Hair Books, 1970.
The Finger: Poems 1966–1969. London: Calder and Boyers, 1970.
As Now It Would Be Snow. Los Angeles: Black Sparrow Press, 1970.
St. Martin's. Los Angeles: Black Sparrow Press, 1971.
A Day Book. New York: Scribner's, 1972.
Listen. Los Angeles: Black Sparrow Press, 1972.
Notebook. New York: Bouwerie Editions, 1972.
Presences: A Text for Marisol. New York: Scribner's, 1976.

SELECT BIBLIOGRAPHY

A Sense of Measure. London: Calder and Boyars, 1973.
His Idea. Toronto: Coach House, 1973.
For My Mother. Knotting, England: Sceptre Press, 1973
The Class of '47. New York: Bouwerie Editions, 1973.
Thirty Things. Los Angeles: Black Sparrow Press, 1974.
Backwards. Knotting, England: Sceptre Press, 1975.
Away. Santa Barbara, Calif.: Black Sparrow Press, 1976.
Hello. Christchurch, New Zealand: Hawk Press. 1976.
Selected Poems. New York: Scribner's, 1976.
Mabel: A Story and Other Prose. London: Marion Boyars, 1976.
Myself. Knotting, England: Sceptre Press, 1977
Thanks. Old Deerfield, Mass.: Deerfield Press, 1977.
Desultory Days. Knotting, England: Sceptre Press, 1978
Hello: A Journal. New York: New Directions, 1978; London: Marion Boyars, 1978.
Later. West Branch, Iowa: Toothpaste, 1978; New York: New Directions, 1979.
"Was That a Real Poem" and Other Essays. Bolinas, Calif.: Four Seasons, 1979.
Corn Close. Knotting, England: Sceptre Books, 1980.
Mother's Voice. Santa Barbara, Calif.: Am Here, 1981.
The Collected Poems: 1945–1975. Berkeley: University of California, 1982.
Echoes. West Branch, Iowa: Toothpaste, 1982.
A Calendar. West Branch, Iowa: Coffee House, 1984.

SELECT BIBLIOGRAPHY

The Collected Prose. New York and London: Marion Boyars, 1984. Reissued, Berkeley and Los Angeles: University of California Press, 1988.
Memories. Durham, England: Pig Press, 1984.
Memory Gardens. New York: New Directions, 1986.
Mirrors. New York: New Directions, 1988.
The Collected Essays. Berkeley and Los Angeles: University of California Press, 1989.
Autobiography. Madras and New York: Hanuman, 1990.
(With Irving Layton). *Irving Layton and Robert Creeley: The Complete Correspondence, 1953–1978.* Ed. Ekbert Faas and Sabrina Reed. Montreal and Kingston: McGill-Queens University Press, 1990.
Windows. New York: New Directions, 1990.
Gnomic Verses. La Laguna, Tenerife: Zasterle, 1991.
Selected Poems. Berkeley: University of California Press, 1991.
Robert Creeley and the Genius of the American Commonplace. Ed. Tom Clark. New York: New Directions, 1993.

Interviews

Creeley, Robert. *Contexts of Poetry: Interviews 1961–1971.* Ed. Donald Allen. Bolinas, Calif.: Four Seasons Foundation, 1973.

SELECT BIBLIOGRAPHY

Elliott, David L. "An Interview with Robert Creeley." *Sagetrieb* 10 (Spring/Fall 1991): 45–65.

Gerber, Phillip L., and Jerome Mazzaro. "From the Forest of Language: A Conversation with Robert Creeley." *Athanor* 4 (Spring 1973): 9–15.

Jackson, Richard. "Projecting the Literal Word." *Acts of the Mind: Conversations with Contemporary Poets.* Tuscaloosa: University of Alabama Press, 1983. 164–71.

Packard, William. "Robert Creeley." *The Poet's Craft.* New York: Paragon, 1987. 153–77.

See also the special Creeley issues of *Sagetrieb* and *Boundary 2,* listed below, and Ekbert Faas, *Towards a New American Poetics,* above.

Works about Creeley

Bibliographies

Fox, Willard, III. *Robert Creeley, Edward Dorn, and Robert Duncan: A Reference Guide.* Boston: G. K. Hall, 1989. Meticulous primary and secondary bibliographies through 1987.

Murray, Timothy, and Stephen Boardway. "Year by Year Bibliography of Robert Creeley." In *Robert Creeley: The Poet's Workshop.* Ed. Carroll F. Terrell. Orono, Maine: National Poetry Foundation, 1984. Lists both periodical and book publications.

SELECT BIBLIOGRAPHY

Prestianni, Vincent. "Robert Creeley: An Analytic Bibliography of Bibliographies." *Sagetrieb* 10 (Spring/Fall 1991): 209–13.

Books

Edelberg, Cynthia Dubin. *Robert Creeley's Poetry: A Critical Introduction.* Albuquerque: University of New Mexico Press, 1978. Survey of the poetry with biographical data.

Ford, Arthur Lewis. *Robert Creeley.* Boston: Twayne, 1978. Introductory survey; attention to influences, biography.

Terrell, Carroll F., ed. *Robert Creeley: The Poet's Workshop.* Orono, Maine: National Poetry Foundation, 1984. Interviews, critical commentary, and a bibliography; an essential volume for any student of Creeley's work.

Wilson, John, ed. *Robert Creeley's Life and Work: A Sense of Increment.* Ann Arbor: University of Michigan Press, 1987. An extensive compilation of commentaries on Creeley's work by more than three dozen poets, critics, and scholars. An excellent place to begin any survey of criticism on Creeley.

Sections of Books

Altieri, Charles. *Self and Sensibility in Contemporary American Poetry.* Cambridge: Cambridge University Press, 1984. Postmodernist character of the work; Olson's influence.

SELECT BIBLIOGRAPHY

Fredman, Stephen. *Poet's Prose: The Crisis in American Verse.* Cambridge and New York: Cambridge University Press, 1983. Prose structure, especially in *Presences.*

Hass, Robert. "Creeley: His Metric." *Twentieth Century Pleasures: Prose on Poetry.* New York: Ecco, 1984. 150–60. Speculative essay on origins and character of Creeley's metrics.

Paul, Sherman. *The Lost America of Love: Rereading Robert Creeley, Edward Dorn, and Robert Duncan.* Baton Rouge: Louisiana State University Press, 1981. Commentary on several Creeley poems with attention to biographical context.

von Hallberg, Robert. *American Poetry and Culture, 1945–1980.* Cambridge: Harvard University Press, 1985. Particular attention to Creeley's style and the early work.

Special Journal Issues

Boundary 2, 6.3–7.1 (Spring/Fall 1978). Works by Creeley; important interview with Creeley by William V. Spanos, "Talking with Creeley"; William V. Spanos, "'The fact of *firstness*': A Preface"; George Butterick, "Olson and Creeley: The Beginning"; Michael Rumaker, "Robert Creeley at Black Mountain"; Paul Mariani, "'Fire of a very real order': Creeley and Williams"; William Sylvester, "Robert Creeley's Poetics: 'I know that I hear you' "; Robert Kern, "Composition as Recognition:

SELECT BIBLIOGRAPHY

Robert Creeley and Postmodern Poetics"; Robert Duncan, "After *For Love*"; Kenneth Cox, "Address and Posture in the Early Poetry of Robert Creeley"; Samuel Moon, "The Springs of Action: A Psychological Portrait of Robert Creeley"; Cynthia Dubin Edelberg, "Robert Creeley's *Words:* The Comedy of the Intellect"; Linda W. Wagner, "Creeley's Late Poems: Contexts"; John Vernon, "'The cry of its own occasion': Robert Creeley"; Robert Duncan, "A Reading of *Thirty Things*"; Peter Quartermain, "Robert Creeley: What Counts"; Paul Diehl, "The Literal Activity of Robert Creeley"; William Navero, "Robert Creeley: Close"; Albert Cook, "Reflections on Creeley"; Robert von Hallberg, "Robert Creeley and the Pleasure of System"; Sherman Paul, "Rereading Creeley"; Robert Grenier, "A Packet for Robert Creeley"; Allen Ginsberg, "On Creeley's Ear Mind"; Tom Clark, "'Desperate perhaps, and even foolish / but God knows useful': Creeley and the Experience of Space"; Duncan McNaughton, "Bullshitting About Creeley"; Warren Tallman, "Haw: A Dream for Robert Creeley"; Nathaniel Mackey, "*The Gold Diggers:* Projective Prose"; Marjorie Perloff, "Four Times Five: Robert Creeley's *The Island*"; Charles Altieri, "Placing Creeley's Recent Work: A Poetics of Conjecture"; Davidson, Michael, "The Presence of the Present: Morality and the Problem of Value in Robert Creeley's Recent Prose."

SELECT BIBLIOGRAPHY

Sagetrieb 1 (Winter 1982). All critical and scholarly essays are reprinted in Terrell, ed., *Robert Creeley: The Poet's Workshop.* Also includes poems by Creeley and others.

Articles

Watten, Barrett, Richard Blevens, Alan Davies, Susan Howe, and Ted Pearson. "Robert Creeley and the Politics of Person." *Poetics Journal* 9 (1991): 138–65. A series of lectures delivered at the St. Mark's Poetry Project (New York City) in 1990.

Works by Robert Duncan

Books

Heavenly City, Earthly City. Berkeley, Calif.: Bern Porter, 1947.
Poems 1948–49. Berkeley, Calif.: Berkeley Miscellany Editions, 1949.
Medieval Scenes. San Francisco: Centaur, 1950.
Caesar's Gate: Poems 1949–1950. Palma de Mallorca: Divers, 1955.
Letters: Poems MCMLIII–MCMLVI. Highlands, N.C.: Jargon, 1958.
Selected Poems. San Francisco: City Lights, 1959.
The Opening of the Field. New York: Grove, 1960.

SELECT BIBLIOGRAPHY

Faust Foutu: A Comic Masque. Stinson Beach, Calif.: Enkidu Surogate, 1960.
As Testimony: The Poem and the Scene. San Francisco: White Rabbit, 1964.
Roots and Branches. New York: Charles Scribner's Sons, 1964.
Writing Writing: a Composition Book: Stein Imitations. Albuquerque, N.M.: Sumbooks, 1964.
Medea at Kolchis: The Maiden Head. Berkeley, Calif.: Oyez, 1965.
Of the War: Passages 22–27. Berkeley, Calif.: Oyez, 1966.
The Years as Catches: First Poems (1939–1946). Berkeley, Calif.: Oyez, 1966.
A Book of Resemblance: Poems: 1950–1953. New Haven: Henry Wenning, 1966.
Bending the Bow. New York: New Directions, 1968.
Derivations: Selected Poems 1950–1956. London: Fulcrum, 1968.
The First Decade: Selected Poems 1940–1950. London: Fulcrum, 1968.
The Truth & Life of Myth: An Essay in Essential Autobiography. New York: House of Books, 1968.
Caesar's Gate. Berkeley, Calif.: Sand Dollar, 1972. Expanded edition of the text published in 1955.
(with Jack Spicer) *An Ode and Arcadia.* Berkeley, Calif.: Ark, 1974.
Medieval Scenes: 1950 and 1959. Kent, Ohio: Kent State University Libraries, 1978.

SELECT BIBLIOGRAPHY

Ground Work: Before the War. New York: New Directions, 1984.

Fictive Certainties. New York: New Directions, 1985.

Ground Work II: In the Dark. New York: New Directions, 1987.

(With H. D.) *A Great Admiration: H. D./Robert Duncan: Correspondence 1950–1961.* Venice, Calif.: Lapis, 1992.

Robert Duncan: Drawings and Decorated Books. N.p.: Rose Books, 1992.

Selected Poems. Ed. Robert Bertholf. New York: New Directions, 1993.

Audit 4 (1967) Duncan and Robin Blaser's respective translations of Gérard de Nerval's *Les Chimères.* Extensive Duncan commentary on his poetics.

"The H. D. Book": Part I, Chapter 1, *Coyote's Journal* 5/6 (1966): 8–31; 2: *Coyote's Journal* 8 (1967): 27–35; 3 and 4: *Tri-Quarterly* 12 (Spring 1968): 67–98; 5: *Stony Brook* 1/2 (Fall 1968): 4–19; 6 (part one): *Caterpillar* 1 (October 1967): 6–29; 6 (part two): *Caterpillar* 2 (January 1968): 125–54. Part II, chapter 1: *Sumac* 1 (Fall 1968): 101–46; 2: *Caterpillar* 6 (January 1969): 16–38; 3: *IO* 6 (Summer 1969): 4; *Caterpillar* 7 (April 1969): 27–60; 5 (section one): *Stony Brook* 3/4 (Fall 1969); 5 (additional material): *Credences* 2 (August 1957): 50–52; 5 (sections previously published in *Stony Brook* and *Credences* plus additional material): *Sagetrieb* 4 (1985):

SELECT BIBLIOGRAPHY

39–86; 6: *Southern Review* 21 (January 1985): 26–48; 7 and 8: *Credences* 2 (August 1957): 53–94; 9: *Chicago Review* 30 (Winter 1979): 37–88; 10: *Ironwood* 22 (1983): 48–64; 11: *Montemora* 8 (1981): 79–113. This work, essential for any student of Duncan, is currently being edited by Robert Bertholf for publication by the University of California Press.

Interviews

Abbott, Steve, and Aaron Shurin. "Interview/Workshop with Robert Duncan." *Soup* 1 (Summer/Fall 1980): 30–57, 79.

———. "Interview: Robert Duncan." *Gay Sunshine* 40/41 (1979): 1–8.

Bowering, George, and Robert Hogg. *Robert Duncan: An Interview*. Toronto: Coach House, 1971.

Cohn, Jack R., and Thomas J. O'Donnell. "An Interview with Robert Duncan." *Contemporary Literature* 21 (Autumn 1980): 513–48.

———. "'The Poetry of Unevenness': An Interview with Robert Duncan." *Credences* n.s. 3 (Spring 1985): 91–111.

Duncan, Robert, and Michael McClure. "In Interview." *Conjunctions* 7 (1985): 69–86.

Hamalian, Linda. "Robert Duncan on Kenneth Rexroth." *Conjunctions* 4 (1983): 85–95.

SELECT BIBLIOGRAPHY

Kamenetz, Rodger. "Realms of Being: An Interview with Robert Duncan." *Southern Review* 21 (January 1985): 5–25.

Mesch, Howard. "Robert Duncan's Interview." *Unmuzzled Ox* 14 (1976): 79–96.

Nicosia, Gerald. "'The Closeness of Mind': An Interview with Robert Duncan." *Unspeakable Visions of the Individual* 12 (1982): 13–27.

Power, Kevin. "A Conversation with Robert Duncan." *Revista Canaria de Estudios Ingleses* 4 (April 1982): 71–106.

Vance, Eugene, and David Schaff. "On Poetry." *Yale Reports* 328 (1964): 1–9.

See also special Duncan issue of *Sagetrieb,* listed below, and Faas, *Towards a New American Poetics,* above.

Works about Duncan

Bibliographies

Bertholf, Robert. *Robert Duncan: A Descriptive Bibliography.* Santa Rosa, Calif.: Black Sparrow Press, 1986.

Fox, Willard, III. *Robert Creeley, Edward Dorn, and Robert Duncan: A Reference Guide.* Boston: G. K. Hall, 1989. Meticulous primary and secondary bibliographies through 1987.

SELECT BIBLIOGRAPHY

Biography

Faas, Ekbert. *Young Robert Duncan: Portrait of the Poet as Homosexual in Society.* Santa Barbara, Calif.: Black Sparow Press, 1983. Useful source for background information; includes reprints of a number of important early essays, particularly "The Homosexual in Society."

Books

Bertholf, Robert J., and Ian W. Reid. *Robert Duncan: Scales of the Marvelous.* New York: New Directions, 1979. Includes reminiscences, bibliography, and commentary. Critical articles include Jayne L. Walker, "Exercises in Disorder: Duncan's Imitations of Gertrude Stein"; Don Byrd, "The Question of Wisdom as Such"; Michael Davidson, "A Book of First Changes: *The Opening of the Field* "; Eric Mottram, "Heroic Survival Through Ecstatic Form: Robert Duncan's *Roots and Branches*"; Thom Gunn, "Homosexuality in Robert Duncan's Poetry"; Ian W. Reid, "Robert Duncan and the Power to Cohere"; Sean Golden, "Duncan's Celtic Mode"; Mark Johnson and Robert DeMott, "'An Inheritance of Spirit': Robert Duncan and Walt Whitman."

Johnson, Mark Andrew. *Robert Duncan.* Boston: Twayne, 1988. A general survey, especially good on Duncan's poetics; close reading of various poems, notably "A Poem Beginning with a Line by Pindar."

SELECT BIBLIOGRAPHY

Mackey, Nathaniel. *Gasire's Lute: Robert Duncan's Vietnam War Poems.* Published serially in *Talisman: A Journal of Contemporary Poetry and Poetics* 5 (Fall 1990): 86–99; 6 (Spring 1991): 141–64; 7 (Fall 1991): 141–66; 8 (Spring 1992): 189–21. Although the specific focus is Duncan's Vietnam War poems, the larger subject is Duncan's poetics. Essential for any student of Duncan's work.

Sections of Books

Davidson, Michael. *The San Francisco Renaissance: Poetics and Community at Mid-Century.* Cambridge and New York: Cambridge University Press, 1989. 125–49 and passim. Duncan's poetics as expression of his sense of community.

Finkelstein, Norman. *The Utopian Moment in Contemporary American Poetry.* Lewisburg, Penn.: Bucknell University Press, 1988. A comparison of Duncan's poetics with Jack Spicer's.

Paul, Sherman. *The Lost America of Love: Rereading Robert Creeley, Edward Dorn, and Robert Duncan.* Baton Rouge: Louisiana State University Press, 1981. Major speculative study, particularly of the work beginning with *The Opening of the Field* and emphasizing the influence of Olson and H. D.

SELECT BIBLIOGRAPHY

Special Journal Issues

Ironwood 22 (1983). An eclectic gathering of works by and about Duncan, including Wendy MacIntyre, "Psyche, Christ and the Poem"; Michael Davidson, "Cave of Resemblances, Cave of Rimes: Tradition and Repetition in Robert Duncan"; Bruce Boone, "Robert Duncan and Gay Community"; Charles Molesworth, "Truth and Life and Robert Duncan"; John Matthias, "Robert Duncan & David Jones: Some Affinities"; Mark Rudman, "Sometimes a Painful Existing"; Mark Johnson, "'Passages': Cross-Sections of the Universe"; John Taggart, "Of the Power of the Word."

Sagetrieb 4 (Fall/Winter 1985). Poems for Duncan by prominent poets, works by Duncan; an interview with Duncan by Michael André Bernstein and Burton Hatlen; Michael André Bernstein, "Robert Duncan: Talent and the Individual Tradition"; Joseph G. Kronick, "Robert Duncan and the Truth That Lies in Myth"; Norman Finkelstein, "Duncan and Spicer on Poetic Composition"; R. S. Hamilton, "After Strange Gods: Robert Duncan Reading Ezra Pound and H. D."; De Villo Sloan, "'Crude Mechanical Access' or 'Crude Personism': A Chronicle of One San Francisco Bay Area Poetry War "; Carl D. Esbjornson, "Tracking the Soul's Truth: Robert Duncan's Revisioning of the Self in *Caesar's Gate*";

SELECT BIBLIOGRAPHY

George F. Butterick, "Seraphic Predator: A First Reading of Robert Duncan's *Ground Work*"; Thomas Gardner, "'Where We Are': A Reading of *Passages* 1–12."

Articles

Bertholf, Robert J. "Shelley, Stevens, and Duncan: The Poetry of Approximations." *Artful Thunder: Versions of the Romantic Tradition in American Literature.* Ed. Robert J. DeMott and Sanford E. Marovitz. Kent, Ohio: Kent State University Press, 1975. Duncan as romantic.

Mackey, Nathaniel. "The World-Poem in Microcosm: Robert Duncan's 'The Continent.'" *ELH* 47 (Fall 1980): 595–618. An intensive reading, locating the poem in terms of structure, theme, myth.

Michaelson, Peter. "A Materialist Critique of Robert Duncan's Grand Collage." *Boundary 2,* 8 (Winter 1980): 21–43. Duncan as idealist.

Olson, Charles. "Against Wisdom as Such." *Black Mountain Review* 1 (Spring 1954): 35–39. Olson's misreading of Duncan; see Duncan chapter for summary and discussion.

Quasha, George. "Duncan Reading." *Credences* 8/9 (1980): 162–75. Duncan's poetics dependent on his reading; his work as a dialectical extension of his reading.

SELECT BIBLIOGRAPHY

Works by Charles Olson

Books

Spanish Speaking Americans in the War. Washington, D.C.: Office of the Coordinator of Inter-American Affairs, 1943.

Call Me Ishmael. New York: Reynal and Hitchcock, 1947.

X & Y. Washington, D.C.: Black Sun, 1948.

In Cold Hell, In Thicket. Palma de Mallorca: Divers, 1953.

The Maximus Poems: 1–10. Stuttgart: Jonathan Williams, 1953.

Mayan Letters. Ed. Robert Creeley. Palma de Mallorca: Divers, 1953.

The Maximus Poems: 11–22. Stuttgart: Jonathan Williams, 1956.

O'Ryan. San Francisco: White Rabbit, 1958.

The Distances. New York: Grove, 1960.

The Maximus Poems. New York: Jargon/Corinth, 1960.

A Bibliography on America for Ed Dorn. San Francisco: Four Seasons Foundation, 1964.

Human Universe and Other Essays. Ed. Donald Allen. San Francisco: Auerhahn, 1965.

Proprioception. San Francisco: Four Seasons Foundation, 1965.

SELECT BIBLIOGRAPHY

Reading at Berkeley. Bolinas, Calif.: Coyote, 1966.
Selected Writings. Ed. Robert Creeley. New York: New Directions, 1966.
Maximus Poems IV, V, VI. London: Cape Goliard; New York: Grossman, 1968.
Pleistocene Man. Buffalo, N.Y.: Institute of Further Studies, 1968.
Casual Mythology. San Francisco: Four Seasons Foundation, 1969.
Letters for Origin: 1950–1956. Ed. Albert Glover. New York: Grossman, 1970.
The Special View of History. Ed. Ann Charters. Berkeley, Calif.: Oyez, 1970.
Poetry and Truth: The Beloit Lectures and Poems. Ed. George F. Butterick. San Francisco: Four Seasons Foundation, 1971.
Archaeologist of Morning. London: Cape Goliard, 1970; New York: Grossman, 1971.
Additional Prose: A Bibliography on America, Proprioception, & Other Notes and Essays. Ed. George F. Butterick. Bolinas, Calif.: Four Seasons Foundation, 1974.
The Maximus Poems: Volume Three. Ed. Charles Boer and George F. Butterick. New York: Grossman, 1975.
The Post Office: A Memoir of His Father. Bolinas, Calif.: Grey Fox, 1975.
The Fiery Hunt and Other Plays. Ed. George F. Butterick. Bolinas, Calif.: Four Seasons, 1977.

SELECT BIBLIOGRAPHY

Muthologos: The Collected Lectures & Interviews. 2 vols. Ed. George F. Butterick. Bolinas, Calif.: Four Seasons Foundation, 1978–79.

(With Robert Creeley.)*Charles Olson and Robert Creeley: The Complete Correspondence.* Ed. George F. Butterick and Richard Blevens. Santa Barbara, Calif.: Black Sparrow Press, 1980- (Volumes I-IX have appeared to date.)

The Maximus Poems. Ed. George F. Butterick. Berkeley and Los Angeles: University of California Press, 1983.

The Collected Poems of Charles Olson. Ed. George F. Butterick. Berkeley and Los Angeles: University of California Press, 1987.

(With Cid Corman). *Charles Olson & Cid Corman: Complete Correspondence: 1950–1964.* 2 vols. Ed. George Evans. Orono, Maine: National Poetry Foundation, 1987–1991.

A Nation of Nothing but Poetry: Supplementary Poems. Santa Rosa, Calif.: Black Sparrow Press, 1989,

(With Edward Dahlberg). *In Love, In Sorrow: The Complete Correspondence of Charles Olson and Edward Dahlberg.* New York: Paragon, 1990.

Selected Poems. Ed. Robert Creeley. Berkeley: University of California Press, 1993.

Interviews

See Olson, *Muthologos: The Collected Lectures & Interviews,* above.

SELECT BIBLIOGRAPHY

Works about Olson

Bibliographies

McPheron, William. *Charles Olson, the Critical Reception, 1941–1983: A Bibliographic Guide.* New York: Garland, 1986. Comprehensive guide to secondary materials.

Prestianni, Vincent. "An Analytical Bibliography of Bibliographies and Selective Checklist of Special Collections, Textual Studies, and Miscellanea." *Sagetrieb* 11 (Spring/Fall 1992): 229–34.

Biographies

Boer, Charles. *Charles Olson in Connecticut.* Chicago: Swallow, 1975. An account of Olson's last months.

Cech, John. *Charles Olson and Edward Dahlberg: A Portrait of a Friendship.* Victoria, B.C.: English Literary Studies, 1982. Dahlberg as seminal influence on Olson's early development.

Clark, Tom. *Charles Olson: The Allegory of a Poet's Life.* New York: Norton, 1991. Major biography; essential for background data.

Seelye, Catherine, ed. *Charles Olson & Ezra Pound: An Encounter at St. Elizabeths.* New York: Grossman, 1975.

SELECT BIBLIOGRAPHY

Books

Bollobas, Eniko. *Charles Olson.* New York: Twayne, 1992. Introductory survey.

Butterick, George F. *A Guide to the Maximus Poems of Charles Olson.* Berkeley and Los Angeles: University of California Press, 1978. Indispensable resource.

Byrd, Don J. *Charles Olson's Maximus.* Urbana: University of Illinois Press, 1980. A poet's close reading of the work.

Christensen, Paul. *Charles Olson: Call Him Ishmael.* Austin: University of Texas Press, 1979. Major study: Olson in relation to other Black Mountain poets; survey of the work.

Charters, Ann. *Olson/Melville: A Study in Affinity.* Berkeley, Calif.: Oyez, 1968. Olson's debt to Melville's notion of space.

Halden-Sullivan, Judith. *The Topology of Being: The Poetics of Charles Olson.* New York: Peter Lang, 1991. Heideggerian analysis.

Merrill, Thomas F. *The Poetry of Charles Olson: A Primer.* Newark: University of Delaware Press, 1982. Good general survey.

Paul, Sherman. *Olson's Push.* Baton Rouge: Louisiana State University Press, 1978. Sympathetic study establishing Olson's context, particularly in terms of his American roots.

SELECT BIBLIOGRAPHY

Stein, Charles. *The Secret of the Black Chrysanthemum.* Barrytown, N.Y.: Station Hill, 1987. Olson's Jungian context.

von Hallberg, Robert. *Charles Olson: The Scholar's Art.* Cambridge: Harvard University Press, 1978. Especially good in tracing Olson's sources.

Sections of Books

Altieri, Charles. *Enlarging the Temple: New Directions in American Poetry During the 1960s.* Lewisburg, Penn.: Bucknell University Press, 1979. Olson as poet of immanence.

Bernstein, Michael André. "The Maximus Poems." *The Tale of the Tribe: Ezra Pound and the Modern Verse Epic.* Princeton: Princeton University Press, 1980. 227–70. Olson's *Maximus Poems* as "modern verse epic" compared with work of Williams and Pound.

Bové, Paul A. "The Particularities of Tradition: History and Locale in *The Maximus Poems.*" *Deconstructive Poetics: Heidegger and Modern American Poetry.* New York: Columbia University Press, 1980. 217–99. Parallels between Olson and Heidegger.

Journal Devoted to Olson

The Journal of the Charles Olson Archives 1–10 (1974–78). Ed. George F. Butterick. Critical and scholarly articles; original documents.

SELECT BIBLIOGRAPHY

Conniff, Brian. *The Lyric and Modern Poetry: Olson, Creeley, Bunting.* New York: Peter Lang, 1988.

Ross, Andrew. *The Failure of Modernism: Symptoms of American Poetry.* New York: Columbia University Press, 1986.

Watten, Barrett. "Olson in Language: The Politics of Style." *Total Syntax.* Carbondale and Edwardsville: Southern Illinois University Press, 1985. 115–40. Presents the language poet's arguments against Olson's poetics of voice; see also Watten, Barrett. "Olson in Language: Part II." *Writing/Talks.* Ed. Bob Perelman. Carbondale and Edwardsville: Southern Illinois University Press, 1985. 157–65.

Articles

Butterick, George. "Charles Olson's 'The Kingfishers' and the Poetics of Change." *American Poetry* 6 (Winter 1989): 28–59. Identification of Olson's sources and references.

Hatlen, Burton. "Kinesis and Meaning: Charles Olson's 'The Kingfishers' and the Critics." *Contemporary Literature* 30 (Winter 1989): 546–72. The poem in terms of Olson's theories of projective verse.

INDEX

Admiral, Virginia, 131
Albers, Josef, 5, 6–7
Allen, Donald: *The New American Poetry,* 27, 137
Anderson, Sherwood, 95; "Death in the Woods," 95–96
Anger, Kenneth, 127

Baudelaire, Charles, 154, 161
Bedford, Juan Amador, 82
Benson, Steve: *The Busses,* 12
Bentley, Eric, 5
Benton, Thomas Hart, 37
Berkeley Poetry Conference, 71–72
Bernstein, Charles, 84
Bernstein, Michael, 33, 54
Berrigan, Ted: "Things To Do In Providence," 114
Berryman, John, 104
Black Mountain College, 1–11
Black Mountain poetics, 11–21
Black Mountain Review, 9
Blake, William, 19
Blaser, Robin, 123, 139, 157
Blavatsky, Helena Petrovna (Madame Blavatsky), 124, 127, 129
Boehme, Jacob, 19, 128
Bohr, Niels, 33
Borregaard, Ebbe, 5
Bosch, Hieronymus, 159
Breuer, Marcel, 4

INDEX

Browning, Robert, 130–31
Butterick, George, 45, 47–48, 65–66, 67
Byron, George Gordon, Lord, 105

Cage, John, 3
Cassirer, Ernst, 148, 149
Celan, Paul, 161
Clark, Tom, 30, 41–42
Collins, Jess, 127
Coolidge, Clark, 21
Copland, Aaron: *Fanfare for the Common Man,* 37
Cranch, Christopher Pearse: "Correspondences," 20
Creeley, Robert
    and Sherwood Anderson, 95–96
    and mid–century avant–garde, 85–86
    at Black Mountain College, 5, 9
    childhood, 89
    and Emily Dickinson, 87–88, 90–91, 116
    and Ralph Waldo Emerson, 20, 88
    as New England Puritan, 89–90, 108
    and Gertrude Stein, 92–93, 94
    and Henry David Thoreau, 87
    and William Carlos Williams, 81–84, 93–94
    Works
      "The Bed," 105
      "Bookcase," 114
      The Charm, 104
      The Collected Poems of Robert Creeley: 1945–1975, 81
      "The Crisis," 105

INDEX

A Day Book, 111
"The Door," 108
"For Irving," 105
For Love, 104
"Four Years Later," 113
The Gold Diggers, 91, 97, 137
"Helsinki Window," 114–15
"I," 109
"Internals," 110
The Island, 98–100, 103
"Kore," 106
"Love," 105
Mabel: A Story, 100–102, 103, 110
Memory Gardens, 113
"The Mirror," 105
"Mr. Blue," 95, 96–97, 101, 102–103, 105
"A Note on the Objective," 94
"Notes for a New Prose," 93
"Numbers," 112
"Oh Max," 114
"The Pattern," 110
Pieces, 108, 109, 110
"Scales," 113
"The Sentence," 106, 107
"Spring Light," 115
"Three Fate Tales," 98
"Wait For Me," 106
"Waiting," 109
"The Whip," 102, 103

Creeley, Robert: Works (*continued*)
    Windows, 113, 114
    Words, 109, 110
    "Words," 83
Crowley, Aleister, 127
Cunningham, Merce, 3

Dahlberg, Edward, 6, 50; *Do These Bones Live?,* 26
Dante Alighieri, 125, 127, 154, 161; *The Divine Comedy,* 126
Davidson, Michael: *The San Francisco Renaissance,* 133
de Kooning, Willem, 3
Dickinson, Emily, 20, 87–88, 90–91, 116, 119n.16
Doolittle, Hilda (H.D.), 135–39, 143, 154, 155; *Tribute to the Angels,* 136; *Trilogy,* 135–6; *The Walls Do Not Fall,* 135
Dorn, Edward, 5
Dove, Arthur, 37
Duberman, Martin, 7
Duncan, Robert
    and anarchism, 131–32
    at Black Mountain College, 5;
    childhood, 124
    and Ralph Waldo Emerson, 21, 42, 124–25, 129–30, 131
    and Jane Harrison, 149
    and H.D., 135–39
    his homosexuality, 131–33, 134
    and language poets, 14–15
    and Jack Spicer, 139–40
    and Gertrude Stein, 144–45
    and Theosophy and hermeticism, 124–29

INDEX

Works
Adam's Way: A Play upon Theosophical Themes, 154
"After a Long Illness," 162
"After Reading H.D.'s *Hermetic Definitions,*" 155
"Among My Friends Love Is a Great Sorrow," 134
"An African Elegy," 132–33, 137, 143
"An Apollonian Elegy," 134
Bending the Bow, 156, 160, 162
"Bending the Bow," 158
Caesar's Gate, 143–44
Derivations, 144
"An Essay at War," 145–46
"The Fire   Passages 13," 159
"Fragment of an Albigensian Rime," 162
Ground Work: Before the War, 160, 161
Ground Work II: In the Dark, 161, 162
"The H. D. Book," 135–39, 155
Heavenly City, Earthly City, 133
"The Helmet of Goliath," 140–41, 144
"The Homosexual in Society," 132
"I Am a Most Fleshly Man," 134
Letters, 10, 137, 146–48, 161
Medieval Scenes, 139–41, 144
"My Mother Would Be a Falconress," 149, 158
"Nel Mezzo Del Cammin Di Nostra Vita," 126
"A New Poem (for Jack Spicer)," 125
"Notes on Poetics Regarding Olson's *Maximus,*" 42
"Ode for Dick Brown," 141
"Orders," 158

INDEX

Duncan, Robert: Works (*continued*)
    "Often I Am Permitted To Return to a Meadow," 151
    The Opening of the Field, 10, 11, 66, 137, 148, 151
    "Passages," 158
    "A Poem Beginning with a Line by Pindar," 152–53
    Roots and Branches, 154
    "The Second Night in the Week," 144
    "A Sequence of Poems for H.D.'s Birthday," 154
    "A Seventeenth Century Suite in Homage to the Metaphysical Genius in English Poetry," 125
    "Shadows," 158
    "Stein Imitations," 130, 144–45, 150
    "The Structure of Rime," 104
    "The Structure of Rime I," 152
    "The Structure of Rime II," 152
    "The Structure of Rime XIV," 125
    "Structure of Rime XX," 156
    "Structure of Rime XXIII," 158
    "Thank You for Love," 125
    "Toward the Shaman," 131, 133
    "Treesbank Poems," 133, 142
    Tribunals, 160
    "The Truth and Life of Myth," 148, 150–51, 159
    "Two Presentations," 154
    "The Venice Poem," 141–43, 145, 147
    The Years As Catches: First Poems (1939–1946), 132, 134

Edson, Russell, 5–6
Eisenhower, Dwight David, 71

INDEX

Eisenstein, Sergei, 106
Eliot, T. S., 7, 139; "The Waste Land," 14, 45
Emerson, Ralph Waldo, 3–4, 19–21, 40–44, 63, 64, 68–69, 74, 86, 88, 124–25, 129–30, 131, 140, 141; "Experience," 140; "Fate," 130; "History," 59–60; *Nature,* 19; "The Poet," 18; "Self-Reliance," 8
Euclid, 34
Everson, William, 128, 131

Fabilli, Mary, 131
Faulkner, William, 50
Fearing, Kenneth, 103
Fenollosa, Ernest, 41, 43–44, 50; *The Chinese Written Character as a Medium for Poetry,* 39, 43
Ficino, Marsilio, 127, 160
Freud, Sigmund, 148
Frobenius, Leo, 33
Frost, Robert, 18, 19–20, 84–85, 86–87; "Education by Poetry," 86
Fuller, Buckminster, 3

Ginsberg, Allen, 9, 49, 111
Gray, Francine du Plessix, 5–6, 38
Grenier, Robert, 14, 92
Gropius, Walter, 4

Harris, Mary Emma, 7
Harrison, Leo, 3
Harrison, Jane Ellen, 149, 150
Hartley, George, 16

INDEX

Hass, Robert, 81–82, 83
Hatlen, Burton, 45–46
Hawthorne, Nathaniel, 39
Heisenberg, Werner, 31
Heraclitus, 62, 63, 74
Herbert, George, 161
Herodotus, 62, 70
Hines, Mary Theresa, 38
Hokanson, Robert O'Brien, 65
Holmes, Oliver Wendell, 39
Howe, Susan, 15, 116, 119n.16
Hutson, Richard, 68–69

James, Henry, 18
James, William, 41, 43
Jeffers, Robinson, 128
Jonson, Ben, 161
Jung, Carl Gustav, 64, 128

Kael, Pauline, 131
Kantorowicz, Ernst: *The King's Two Bodies,* 138
Kazin, Alfred, 5
Kenner, Hugh, 43
Kerouac, Jack, 9; "October in the Railroad Earth," 100
Kline, Franz, 3, 85
Kocher, A. Lawrence, 4
Kuberski, Philip, 41

language poets, 11–16, 21
Lawrence, D. H., 138–39; *Etruscan Places,* 60; *Studies in Classic American Literature,* 26

INDEX

Levertov, Denise, 158; "The Shifting," 137
Longfellow, Henry Wadsworth, 39
Lowell, James Russell, 39
Lowell, Robert, 49, 104; "The Quaker Graveyard in Nantucket," 44

Mackey, Nathaniel, 21, 75
Mallarmé, Stéphane, 31, 127, 128
Marisol, 100
Matthiessen, F. O., 25–26, 27, 36–37, 39, 70; *American Renaissance,* 25
Maximus of Tyre, 67
McClure, Michael, 49
Melville, Herman, 25–26, 27–28, 29, 31–33, 36, 39, 40, 41, 74; *Moby-Dick,* 32, 74
Miës van der Rohe, Ludwig, 85
Miller, Henry, 50
Motherwell, Robert, 5

Nerval, Gérard de: *Chimeras,* 123
"New American Story," 92
New Formalists, 18
Notley, Alice, 21

Olson, Charles
    as academic, 26–27, 31–34, 36–37
    at Black Mountain College, 2, 5–11
    childhood, 38
    and Ralph Waldo Emerson, 40–44, 68–69
    and Ernest Fenollosa, 40, 43–44
    and language poets, 11–14

INDEX

Olson, Charles (*continued*)
    and F. O. Matthiessen, 25–26
    and Herman Melville, 27–28, 31–33
    and New England, 38–39
    and politics, 25
    Works
      "Against Wisdom as Such," 9, 17, 75, 122, 126
      Call Me Ishmael, 25–26, 27–28, 74
      The Collected Poems, 66
      "Conqueror," 55
      "Diaries of Death," 39
      "The Escaped Cock: Notes on Lawrence and the Real," 60–61
      "The Growth of Herman Melville, Prose Writer and Poetic Thinker," 31
      "History," 61–62
      "The House," 30
      "Human Universe," 60
      "In Cold Hell, in Thicket," 53
      "The K," 30, 31
      "The Kingfishers," 13, 74, 45–49, 55, 104
      "Letter for Melville 1951," 31, 75
      "Lower Field—Enniscorthy," 57
      "A Lustrum for You, E. P.," 54
      The Maximus Poems, 11, 12, 17, 28, 30–31, 33, 48, 55, 63, 64, 66–75
      A Nation of Nothing but Poetry, 66
      "The Praises," 57
      "Projective Verse," 30, 42, 44, 49–52, 106–107, 111, 137, 146, 150

INDEX

    Spanish Speaking Americans in the War, 39
    The Special View of History, 8, 27, 62–65, 68, 75
    "There Was a Youth Whose Name Was Thomas
        Granger," 55
    "This Is Yeats Speaking," 54
    "To Gerhardt," 58
    "La Torre," 44–45
    "White Horse," 28
    X&Y, 10
Oppenheimer, Joel, 6

Patchen Kenneth, 103, 134–35
Paul, Sherman, 42–43, 59, 78n.17; *Emerson's Angle of Vision,*
    42; *Olson's Push,* 42
Perloff, Marjorie, 13, 51
Perse, St.-John, 155
Petrarch, 108
Pico della Mirandola, 127
Piero di Cosimo, 159
Plath, Sylvia, 17
Pollock, Jackson, 85
Pound, Ezra, 33–34, 43, 51, 53–56, 58, 125, 134, 139, 141,
    142; *Cantos,* 58, 149
Prynne, Jeremy, 49

Rahv, Philip, 18
Ransom, John Crowe, 132
Rauschenberg, Robert, 3
Reimann, Georg Friedrich Bernhard, 34

INDEX

Rexroth, Kenneth, 103, 128, 156, 160; *In What Hour,* 134; *The Phoenix and the Tortoise,* 134; *The Signature of All Things,* 134
Rice, Dan, 3
Rice, John Andrew, 1–5, 22n.1
Rice, William C., 3
Richards, M. C., 2
Rilke, Ranier Maria, 127, 131
Rodilla, Simon, 126
Roethke, Theodore, 9
Roosevelt, Franklin Delano, 25, 53
Rosenthal, M. L., 111
Rukeyser, Muriel, 50, 103
Rumaker, Michael, 6
Rumi, 161

San Francisco Theater Project, 11
Sandburg, Carl, 37
Saroyan, William, 50; "American Qualities," 50
Schubert, Franz, 158
Sealts, Merton M., Jr., 33
Sedgwick, William Ellery, 39
Shahn, Ben, 5, 37
Shakespeare, William, 72, 124; *King Lear,* 32; *Othello,* 142; *The Tempest,* 127
Shelley, Percy Bysshe, 17, 125, 154
Silliman, Ron, 14
Snyder, Gary, 156
Sobin, Gustaf, 20, 75, 103

INDEX

Spicer, Jack, 72, 125, 128–29, 139; *After Lorca,* 139, 154; *Imaginary Elegies,* 157
Stein, Gertrude, 41, 43, 92–93, 94, 95, 137, 144, 146, 147; *Three Lives,* 92
Stravinsky, Igor: *The Poetics of Music,* 141
Swedenborg, Emanuel, 19, 86, 124
Symmes, Edwin and Minnehaha, 124

Tallman, Warren, 93
Taylor, Edward, 90, 108
Theosophy, 124, 125–29
Thomas, Dylan, 9
Thomson, J. A. K.: *The Art of the Logos,* 61
Thoreau, Henry David, 20, 34–35, 39, 41, 70, 86, 87, 90, 117, 127, 131; *The Maine Woods,* 34; *Walden,* 8, 34
Thucydides, 59, 62
Tudor, David, 3

Walker, Jayne L., 145
Watten, Barrett, 11–123, 115–16, 145; *Total Syntax,* 12
Whitehead, Alfred North: *Aims of Education,* 128; *Process and Reality,* 16, 62–63
Whitman, Walt, 20, 26, 29, 39, 41, 90, 105–106, 117, 151, 160
Wilbur, Richard, 18, 49, 104
Williams, William Carlos, 49, 51, 53, 57–58, 81, 84, 93, 103, 157; *The Embodiment of Knowledge,* 57; *In the American Grain,* 26, "The Lily," 81–82; *Paterson,* 66; *The Wedge,* 86
Winthrop, John, 108
Wolfe, Thomas, 50

INDEX

Wolpe, Stefan, 3
Wright, Frank Lloyd, 37

Yates, Frances, 124
Yeats, William Butler, 127, 131

Zukofsky, Louis: *A,* 14; *80 Flowers,* 15

**NORTH CAROLINA ROOM
NEW HANOVER COUNTY PUBLIC LIBRARY**